Enjoying God

Discovering the Greatest of All Pleasures

Rick Howe

Rick Howe

Books by Rick Howe

Path of Life: Finding the Joy You've Always Longed For, 2012, University Ministries Press Revised Edition, 2017. 279 pages.

River of Delights: Quenching Your Thirst For Joy, Volume 1, 2015, University Ministries Press Revised Edition, 2017. 230 pages.

River of Delights: Quenching Your Thirst For Joy, Volume 2, 2015, University Ministries Press Revised Edition, 2017. 250 pages.

Living Waters: Daily Refreshment for Joyful Living, 2017, University Ministries Press. 393 pages.

Reasons of the Heart: Joy and the Rationality of Faith, 2017, University Ministries Press. 250 pages.

For Small Group Studies

Enjoying God: Discovering the Greatest of All Pleasures, University Ministries Press, 2017. 122 pages.

Love's Delights: The Joys of Marriage and Family, University Ministries Press, 2017. 104 pages.

Sacred Patterns: Work, Rest, and Play in a Joyful Vision of Life, University Ministries Press, 2017. 122 pages.

Kingdom Manifesto: A Call to Joyful Activism, University Ministries Press, 2017. 104 pages.

Joy and the Problem of Evil, University Ministries Press, Boulder, 2017. 122 pages.

For more information, visit www.rickhowe.org.

UNIVERSITY MINISTRIES PRESS
BOULDER, COLORADO

Enjoying God has been drawn from the first six chapters of Rick Howe: *Rivers of Delight: Quenching Your Thirst For Joy, Volume 1* (Boulder, CO: University Ministries Press, 2017).
Used by Permission.

ISBN: 978-0-9962696-7-4

ABBREVIATIONS

KJV	King James Version
NASB	New American Standard Bible
NIV	New International Version of the Bible
NRSV	New Revised Standard Version Bible
RSV	Revised Standard Version of the Bible

Contents

AUTHOR'S NOTE

Enjoying God is drawn from the first six chapters of *River of Delights: Quenching Your Thirst for Joy, Volume 1.*

There are many footnotes in *Enjoying God.* If texts of Scripture are not given in full in the main body of a chapter, they have been included in the footnotes to make it possible for you to read the book without the extra chore of looking them up yourself. There are also many references to other works, as well as my own comments. My suggestion is that you read the text first without interacting with the footnotes in order to trace the flow of thought without interruption, and then read it again with the footnotes.

The "Questions for Thought and Discussion" for each chapter reflect my hope that you will study this book with others, my belief that learning in community is the best way to learn, and my prayer that God will use this book to create communities of joy for the advancement of his Kingdom.

PREFACE

An apocalyptic foreboding has many in its grip, strengthened by endless newsfeeds and broadcasts featuring economic woes, violence, terrorism, wars and threats of war, corruption in high places, depletion of energy resources, global climate change, natural catastrophes, pestilence, and toxins in our environment and our food.

No wonder words like *anxiety, depression, melancholy, and stress* are used to describe our generation! Historians in the future might well call ours *The Age of Prozac.* Depressive disorders are widespread. The pharmaceutical industry has grown rich on them.

The fact that this emotional epidemic grows unabated should signal the possibility that we have misdiagnosed and mistreated the problem. I don't deny that there are frightening factors behind our personal angst and cultural malaise, but I believe that there is an underlying cause that we ignore at our own greater peril. We are disoriented and dysfunctional. We are disoriented because we have removed God from our vision of life, and dysfunctional because we vainly attempt to live without him. Much else (economic woes, violence, toxins in our environment, *et al*) results directly or indirectly from this.

"A joyful heart is a good medicine."[1] This was once proverbial wisdom. It is true because joy connects us with God, and that is the healthiest place for us to be. Dallas Willard wrote, "Full joy is our first line of defense against weakness, failure, and disease of mind and body."[2] Peter Kreeft says much the same: "A joyful spirit inspires joyful feelings and even a more psychosomatically healthy body. (For example, we need less sleep when we have joy and have more resistance to all kinds of diseases from colds to cancers.)"[3] This ancient wisdom deserves a revival in our day. In fact, it is our only hope.

The premises of this book are that joy links us with God, it can touch and transform every dimension of our lives, and we will flourish only as we position ourselves to receive this gift from Him.

Let's listen in on the worship of the Psalmist:

> Your steadfast love, O LORD, extends to the heavens,
> your faithfulness to the clouds.
> Your righteousness is like the mountains of God;
> your judgments are like the great deep;
> man and beast you save, O LORD.
> How precious is your steadfast love, O God!
> The children of mankind take refuge in the shadow of your wings.
> They feast on the abundance of your house,
> and you give them drink from the river of your delights.
> For with you is the fountain of life;
> in your light do we see light. (Psalm 36:5-9)

If you are open to the Voice that beckons in these words, welcome to *Enjoying God*!

CHAPTER 1

THE GREATEST OF ALL PLEASURES

Imagine a room with high-backed chairs around a great oaken table, set with plates, silverware, goblets, and bowls. There are pitchers filled with fruity refreshment, and baskets with rolls hot from an oven. The aroma fills your senses and draws you in. You can almost taste the pastry and melting butter. On the other side of a door, partly closed, you hear bustling, merry singing, and the clanking of pots and pans. The wondrous smells of unseen cuisine waft into the room. You can't remember the last time you ate. It must have been ages ago!

You've been invited to a banquet. Take your place at the table and prepare for something exquisite. We will feast from the bounty of God's house. Our drink has been fetched from the river of his delights:

> How precious is your steadfast love, O God!
> The children of mankind take refuge
> in the shadow of your wings.
> They feast on the abundance of your house,
> and you give them drink from the river of your delights.
> (Psalm 36:7-8)

Here is the first and most important thing for you to know in order to fill your hungry, thirsty heart: Joy is the greatest of all pleasures, and the enjoyment of God is the greatest of all joys.[1] Joy is the best gift we can possibly receive, because the Giver offers himself in his gift, and he is supreme.

The enjoyment of God is not only the greatest of all joys, it is the Joy in every joy. Wherever there is true joy, God is in it, whether he is beheld in the enraptured gaze of our hearts, or is the Light by which other pleasures are illumined and experienced as his good gifts.[2] Joy always has to do with God. Always. *Whether we know it or not, our experience of joy in every instance is a connection with God.*[3] If we are held in hushed delight before a forest ablaze with autumn color, we have encountered the Creator in his artistry. If we revel in a sumptuous meal and find ourselves savoring the experience with a thankful heart, we have tasted his goodness. If we find pleasure in people, it is an enjoyment of God mirrored in them,[4] and, among those who are being redeemed, the habitation of God within them.[5]

There is no joy apart from God. It is not even possible. To speak of joy without speaking of God is a desecration of language. If we knew the true nature and dimensions of joy, we would see that it is always, and never less than, our heart's encounter with the Joyful One. Joy is the touch of God. The fragrance of his presence. A glimpse of his beauty. An echo of his voice.[6]

To say that we were created for God, and that we were made for joy, is to say the same thing in different ways. In words now famous, Augustine wrote, "You have formed us for yourself, and our hearts are restless until they find rest in You."[7] We are vagabonds, wandering restively in pursuit of something that beckons and yet eludes us until we find our hearts' true home in God. Pascal saw our quest for joy ending here:

> There once was in man a true happiness of which there now remain to him only the mark and empty trace, which he in vain tries to fill from all his surroundings, seeking from things absent the help he does not obtain in things present. . . . But these are all inadequate, because the infinite abyss can only be filled by an infinite and immutable object, that is to say, only by God himself.[8]

The greatest joy in this world (and the next) is our hearts' delight in God.[9] For those who know it, nothing enriches life more. Nothing pleases more fully. Nothing satisfies the longings of our hearts more profoundly than a joy that is at the same time adoration and awe, reverence and rapture, breath-taking wonder and soul-satisfying pleasure. It is a delight in the beauty, majesty, and splendor of God, and then a joy that so great and glorious a God is ours.[10] The enjoyment of God leaves us incredulous, marveling, "*Surely this is too good to be true!*" But it is supremely good and it is true. It is a pleasure-filled wonder (or wonderful pleasure) that there should be such a God, and even greater pleasure and greater wonder that he offers himself to us for our joy.

ENJOYING GOD FOR WHO HE IS

God's joy, first, is his delight in himself.[11] He enjoys being God. He exults in his excellence. He rejoices in his regal splendor. He takes boundless pleasure in his infinite perfection. It is a good thing for us that he does! There would be no joy anywhere in the universe if he did not. God's joy is the fountain from which our joy flows. Ours is a share in his. Like his, our joy is first a delight in who God is. Not what he does *for* us, but who he is *to* us.[12] Jonathan Edwards wrote of this joy:

> True saints have their minds, in the first place, inexpressibly pleased and delighted with the sweet ideas of the glorious and amiable nature of the things of God. And this is the spring of all their delights, and the cream of all their pleasures; 'tis the joy of their joy. This sweet and ravishing entertainment, they have in viewing the beautiful and delightful nature of divine things, is the foundation of the joy they have afterward in the consideration of their being theirs.[13]

We tend to approach the attributes of God abstractly.[14] Apart from an encounter with God, our systematic theologies make his traits lifeless things to our hearts. Though it is scandalous to do so, we read about the holiness of God with a yawn. Isaiah encountered the Thrice Holy God and fell on his face as a dead man.[15] Though Heaven is appalled at the ingratitude, we take the goodness of God for granted. Barely able to contain himself, the Psalmist cried out, "O taste and see that the LORD is good!"[16] We treat his justice as the duty of deity. Sacred poets saw it inspiring the entire cosmos in a joyous song of praise:

> Say among the nations, "The LORD reigns!
> Yea, the world is established, it shall never be moved;
> he will judge the peoples with equity."
> Let the heavens be glad, and let the earth rejoice;
> let the sea roar, and all that fills it;
> let the field exult, and everything in it!
> Then shall all the trees of the wood sing for joy
> before the LORD, for he comes,
> for he comes to judge the earth.
> He will judge the world with righteousness,
> and the peoples with his truth. (Psalm 96:10-13)

To the astonishment of angels, we argue about divine sovereignty and human freedom. The very thought of a God who in sovereign generosity gives us liberty and in sovereign mercy forgives our sinful use of that gift led the apostle Paul not to debate but to worship:

> O the depth of the riches and the wisdom and knowledge of God!
> How unsearchable are his judgments and how inscrutable his ways!
> "For who has known the mind of the Lord,
> or who has been his counselor?"
> "Or who has given a gift to him
> that he might be repaid?"
> For from him and through him and to him are all things.
> To him be glory for ever. Amen. (Romans 11:33-36)[17]

The attributes of God are not textbook definitions. They are facets of who he is. Dimensions of deity that impinge upon us. Qualities of the One with whom we have to do.[18] We do not experience them in their fullness or crystalline clarity. In our present state we could bear neither. Nevertheless, in ways that are suited to our fallenness and finitude, God discloses himself to us, and in that circle of encounter we discover the joy for which we were made. Daily our hearts then echo the ancient prayer: "Satisfy us in the morning with your steadfast love (an experience of God, and not just a theological idea) so that we may rejoice and be glad all our days."[19]

ENJOYING GOD FOR WHAT HE DOES

God takes pleasure in all that he does and invites us to find our joy here, as well:

> Our God is in the heavens;
> he does all that he *pleases*. (Psalm 115:3)

> Whatever the LORD *pleases*, he does. (Psalm 135:6)
>
> *The LORD was pleased* for his righteousness' sake, to magnify his law and make it glorious. (Isaiah 42:21)
>
> I am the LORD who practices steadfast love, justice and righteousness in the earth; *for in these things I delight,* says the LORD. (Jeremiah 9:24)
>
> I will make with them an everlasting covenant, that I will not turn away from doing good to them; and I will put the fear of me in their hearts, that they may not turn from me. *I will rejoice in doing them good . . . with all my heart and all my soul.* (Jeremiah 32:40-41)[20]

God is always active, which means that his joy in what he does is always full.[21] We have the barest glimpse of the smallest part of what he does in the world, but even this can bring joy. Imagine an awareness of his activity far greater than ours! Jesus saw God's presence and work in the world as no one else ever has:

> Jesus said to them, "Truly, truly, I say to you, the Son can do nothing of his own accord, but only what he sees the Father doing. For whatever the Father does, that the Son does likewise. (John 5:19)
>
> To his eyes this is a God-bathed, and God-permeated world. It is a world filled with a glorious reality, where every component is within the range of God's direct knowledge and control – though he obviously permits some of it, for good reasons, to be for a while otherwise than as he wishes. It is a world that is inconceivably beautiful and good because of God and because God is always in it. It is a world in which God is continually at play and over which he constantly rejoices.[22]

Joy is an interface between our hearts and God's activity in the world. It is a nexus between the two. The greater our knowledge of what God is doing, the greater our opportunities for joy; the greater our joy, the greater our incentive to discover what he is doing in the world.

Jesus invites us to share his vision of the world, and to enter into his joy, "that my joy may be in you and that your joy may be full," he said.[23] We don't need to have his knowledge of God's activity in the world; we need only to place our confidence in him, trust that his vision of the world is true, and ask him to show us more of what he sees.[24] Don't talk yourself out of this joy because it is beyond the boundaries of what you have experienced so far. And don't let others dissuade or discourage you because they are strangers to this. Jesus was not naïve! (If you believe that he was, I'm not sure how you can be his follower.) Your first step into his vision of the world and into his joy may be the prayer, "I believe. Help my unbelief!"[25] He takes pleasure in first steps. Even small steps. You will find joy with each one you take.

JOY IN THE TRIUNE GOD

The Trinity is not a doctrine dropped from the heavens in a theological treatise. It is a truth given in God's self-disclosure: a revelation whose original medium was the teaching of Jesus and the matching experience of his early followers.[26] (Without his teaching, his disciples would not have understood their experience; without their experience, his teaching would have been sounds in the air.)

The threefoldness of the one God was not a matter of theological calculus for our ancient brothers and sisters of faith, but a compelling dimension of their experience of God as he revealed himself to them. They came to know the one true God as Father, Son, and Holy Spirit.[27]

Joy in the Father. Jesus introduced his disciples to the fatherhood of God, and to the joys of knowing him this way. He taught them to address God as *Abba* - the familiar and endearing term of a child for her father.[28] For those men and women the fatherhood of God was not a theological abstraction. It was an experience into which Jesus guided them. In the Father's power they found protection. In his providence they found direction. In his loving care they found supply for their needs. In his wisdom they found guidance for living well. In his Kingdom they found the greatest possible adventure, and the most significant investment of their lives.[29]

Joy in the Son. They discovered, however, that there was more to the fatherhood of God than their monotheistic minds were at first prepared to accept. The One who introduced them to God as their heavenly Father, and whose joy in the Father they shared, claimed deity for himself and called himself the Son.[30] He directed their joy not only to the Father, but to himself: "These things I have spoken to you, that my joy may be in you, and that your joy may be full."[31] Peter Kreeft sees the significance of this: "The man who said he was God also said he was our joy. If this claim is not true, it is the most blasphemous, egotistical, and insane thing ever spoken by human lips. If it is true, then God's single gift for all our desires is his Son. He *is* joy, joy alive and wearing a real human face. . . ." [32]

As unsettling as his claims must have been, his followers were compelled either to reject them or to accept them and make significant theological adjustments.[33] They were faced with the dilemma of dismissing Jesus or including him in their understanding of God. We know the cruciform reaction of their contemporaries. How would his disciples respond?

As they shared life with Jesus, they detected no flaw of sin.[34] As they watched and listened, they saw potency in his words and deeds that they had never witnessed before. When Jesus spoke, uncanny things happened. People were healed. Demons were cast out. The dead were raised to life. Storms were quelled. Multitudes were fed. And then there was his teaching! He stood the rabbinic world on its head, speaking as if he were the Authority above all human authorities.[35] His disciples were astonished as he assumed the divine prerogative of forgiving sin.[36] They were wide-eyed with wonder at his claims to have come from God and to be one with God.[37] They were startled by his declaration to be Lord of the Sabbath[38] and amazed at the unpretentious manner in which he saw himself as Lord of the Great Judgment awaiting all humanity at the end of days.[39] All of this was scandalous. Blasphemous! Or it was a window. A portal to a new but true understanding of God.[40]

As perplexing as these things must have been, his followers also found in Jesus the joy for which they longed, and which they had sought vainly in other things. In time they confessed what they did not fully comprehend, that the one God exists as Father and Incarnate Son.[41] In Jesus, the one God had come among them. To their enjoyment of the Father they were compelled to add a shared joy in the One who was uniquely the Father's Son.

Joy in the Spirit. Their joy and understanding of God became more richly colored and textured on the day of Pentecost when they were gifted and filled with the Holy Spirit.[42] They had been led by Jesus to expect a great event that would take place after his departure from them. He told them that the Spirit of Truth would come, sent by the Father to take his place upon the earth.[43] The Spirit would be distinct from the Son, and yet – in an utter mystery and a wondrous reality – would be the mode by which the risen Christ himself would be present among them.[44]

When that day came, another dimension was added to their joy. They had come to know joy in the Father and joy in the Son. From Pentecost on, they began to know joy in the Holy Spirit. In nuance it was different from the joy they had already learned, and yet it shared a kinship with their joy in the Father and their joy in Jesus. To some who looked on, this pleasure appeared to be the intoxication of wine.[45] To those who knew it in experience, however, it was the presence of the Spirit, welling up within them and overflowing in praise and an undaunted delight in proclaiming what God had done for them in Christ.

They experienced the Spirit as a Coming of Power.[46] A Clothing of Power.[47] They came to know him as Helper in the midst of life's challenges.[48] They discovered him as Teacher and Guide as they explored the new terrain of the Gospel.[49] They recognized him as Pledge and Guarantor, bearing witness with their spirits that they were children of God.[50] They knew him as Herald, inspiring deep within them the exultant cry, "Abba, Father!"[51] They found him to be the Source of their joy, even in the midst of hardship and persecution.[52]

We see a fledgling Trinitarian understanding of God in the benediction of Paul to the church in Corinth: "The grace of the Lord Jesus Christ and the love of God and the fellowship of the Holy Spirit be with you all."[53] This was meaningful to the Corinthian believers because it was true to their experience of God. They understood this way of speaking about God because they, too, had encountered him in these ways. As this joyful experience spread across the ancient world, and more and more came to speak this spiritually formed language, the doctrine of the Trinity emerged.[54]

Trinitarian joy. Augustine knew this joy in the Triune God: "The true objects of enjoyment, then, are the Father and the Son and the Holy Spirit, who are at the same time the Trinity, one Being, supreme above all, and common to all who enjoy Him."[55] I doubt that this three-faceted joy is as common today as Augustine believed it was in his fifth century world. To be generous to our generation, we are further removed from the epic events in the drama of redemption. Less generously (but more tellingly), we pay too little attention to what is already a slighter spiritual experience than our ancient brothers and sisters enjoyed. This is not a delight for debutants. Only serious (not to be mistaken for *somber*) followers of Jesus know it. It is a pleasure that flourishes in thoughtful hearts, in hearts that are habituated in worship of the Father, Son, and Spirit, in hearts that dance to songs of thanksgiving and praise to the Threefold God.

In this circle of encounter with God we discover the robust, three-dimensional joy that enriched the life of the early Church: joy in the Father for his work in creation and redemption, and for his provision and protective care; joy in the Son for his life among us, and for the blessings of salvation purchased through his death and resurrection; and joy in the Spirit who points us daily to Christ, and who dwells within us as an empowering presence and pledge of all that God has in store for us.[56]

Questions for Thought and Discussion

1. If God has created a void within you that only he can fill, in what ways have you tried to fill that emptiness apart from God? With what things? What pursuits? What relationships? How do you see this playing out with your peers?

2. Why is it significant that our joy in God is linked to his joy in himself? Are there obstacles in your understanding of God that keep you from affirming his joy?

3. Why is it important to seek our joy first in who God is, and not what he can do for us? What are the implications of seeing God as a means to our ends, even if it is our own joy?

4. Describe experiences you have had in which you encountered God and became strikingly aware of some facet of his deity, e.g., his holiness, his goodness, his wisdom, his justice.

5. Can you identify nuances of joy in your relationship with God? Joy in the Father? Joy in the Son? Joy in the Spirit? If not, don't be discouraged! Let this be a catalyst for spiritual growth.

CHAPTER 2

JOY AND THE GLORY OF GOD

JOY AND GOD'S SELF-DISCLOSURE

God of glory,[1] King of glory,[2] Father of glory,[3] Majestic Glory.[4] Have you ever heard God addressed with these titles? Have you used them in prayer or in conversation with others? No? But they were given to us in the Scriptures, and they were given for a reason. Not only have they dropped out of our vocabulary of worship and prayer, they have all but vanished from our thoughts of God. We have lost ancient and important truths that were meant to shape our relationship with God, and we have been greatly impoverished as a result.

The glory of God, first, is all that he is in his transcendence over the world. It is his splendor, his magnificence, his majesty, and infinite worth. The glory of God is not a single attribute of God, but his nature in its fullness. In all that he is, God is glorious!

The fitting response of our hearts to the glory of God is reverence, wonder, and awe: a shudder at our own smallness, a shivering sense of the magnitude of God, a trembling delight in the grandeur of our God. Hearts that have been gripped by glory know the tremulous joy that so great a Being exists, and an astonishment-that-takes-one's-breath-away that so great a God invites us to know him and to enjoy him. It is a pleasure that is at once dread and delight, fear and fascination, amazement and adoration. To glorify God, first and foremost, is to acknowledge, confess, celebrate, and live our lives in light of God's glory. This is where joy is found. This is where our hearts discover pleasure in God.[5]

If this were all we knew about God's glory, it would fill our cup. But we must let it overflow, because this is only the truth by half. In the Sacred Word, *glory* not only describes God in himself, but God in his self-disclosure to us.[6] Let's explore this.

God is Spirit.[7] One thing about spirits is that they can't be discovered by our senses. They are invisible to us. In a hymn of praise, Paul wrote, "To the King of ages, immortal, *invisible*, the only God, be honor and glory for ever and ever. Amen."[8] Later in that same letter, he said that no one has ever seen God and no one can see him.[9] It is impossible because of who God is. The invisibility of God is fundamental Christian theology. If you want a visible and tangible deity you will have to find another religion, because Christianity insists that the true God can't be seen with our eyes or detected by our senses.

But that isn't all the Bible says about God. It also says that the invisible God reveals himself to people in visible and tangible ways. God's presence in the world is imperceptible, but the tokens of his presence are not. He dons a robe, as it were, to reveal himself to mortals.[10] The Bible uses the word *glory* to describe his mantle. We can't see God, but we can behold his glory – the visible, tangible manifestation of the invisible, intangible God.[11] This is the second way in which the Bible uses the word *glory* in connection with God. Glory is what we encounter when God reveals himself in perceptible ways.

GOD'S GLORY IN NATURE

The heavens above us and the world around us brim with glory:

> The heavens are telling the glory of God. (Psalm 19:1)
>
> Holy, holy, holy is the LORD of hosts;
> The whole earth is full of his glory. (Isaiah 6:3)

Creation is filled with emblems of God's presence. The heavens are his crest, the earth his throne. His footmarks are everywhere, his fingerprints on all that he has made. If we see the world truly, it is not devoid of God (the mistake of Deism[12]), nor is it God (the error of Pantheism[13]), nor even the body of God (the false view of Panentheism[14]). It is a theater in which God displays his glory.[15]

We can make high stakes mistakes here. Those who venerate nature and bestow upon it the status of deity are in touch with the fact that there is more to the world than meets the eye. At some level they are aware that God is there. But they mistake his glory in the world for an identity with the world, and in doing so worship the creature rather than the Creator, who alone is worthy of praise.[16] If we acknowledge the creaturely status of the world, however, we are invited to enjoy the Creator in it, just as we enjoy a poet in her poem, an artist in his painting, or a composer in his music. Augustine put it this way:

> Let your mind roam through the whole creation; everywhere the created world will cry out to you: "God made me." Whatever pleases you in a work of art brings to your mind the artist who wrought it; much more, when you survey the universe, does the consideration of it evoke praise for its Maker. . . . Now if in considering these creatures of God human language is so at a loss,

> what is it to do in regard to the Creator? When words fail, can aught but triumphant music remain?[17]

BEAUTY AND GLORY

The tangerine beauty of a sunset. The shimmering beauty of moonbeams on a lake. The distant beauty of a star-spangled sky. The brilliant beauty of sun-glistened snow. The lush beauty of a forest canopy. The arid beauty of a desert. The majestic beauty of mountains. The winged beauty of geese in flight. The underwater beauty of coral gardens. The thundering beauty of cascading waterfalls. The lustrous beauty of earthen gems. Beauty in the world is the glory of God.[18]

To learn from Augustine again:

> Question the beauty of the earth, question the beauty of the sea, question the beauty of the air, amply spread around everywhere, question the beauty of the sky, question the serried ranks of the stars, question the sun making the day glorious with is bright beams, question the moon tempering the darkness of the following night with its shining rays, question the animals that move in the waters, that amble about on dry land, that fly in the air . . . . They all answer you, 'Here we are, look; we're beautiful." Their beauty is their confession. Who made these beautiful changeable things, if not one who is beautiful and unchangeable?[19]

The beauty of creation is its confession. Our confession is taking pleasure in its beauty and responding to the Creator in adoration and awe.

I must warn you that there is both pleasure and peril in the beauty of the world: pleasure for those who enjoy it and whose hearts are filled with reverent appreciation, and peril for those who suppress the true significance of beauty and shut God out of their thoughts about the world. The apostle Paul wrote:

> For the wrath of God is revealed from heaven against all ungodliness and unrighteousness of men, who by their unrighteousness suppress the truth. For what can be known about God is plain to them, because God has shown it to them. For his invisible attributes, namely, his eternal power and divine nature, have been clearly perceived, ever since the creation of the world, in the things that have been made. So they are without excuse. For although they knew God, they did not honor him as God or give thanks to him, but they became futile in their thinking, and their foolish hearts were darkened. (Romans 1:18-21)

We are surrounded on all sides by the glory of God in the beauty of his world. There is no escaping it! Our only choice is how we will respond to it. Beauty summons us to open our hearts to our Creator in pleasure and praise. In the beauty of the world God invites us to exalt him by exulting in all that he has made. If we refuse the invitation, beauty will rise in a gallery of witnesses to speak against us on the last day.

DIVINE VISITATIONS

Sometimes in the Scriptures God visits his people in dramatic ways. They see an aura of unearthly light. They become aware of a luminous presence. And they know that they have been visited by Heaven.[20] This, too, is God's glory:

> When Moses came down from Mount Sinai, with the two tablets of the testimony in his hand as he came down from the mountain, Moses did not know that *the skin of his face shone because he had been talking with God.* Aaron and all the people of Israel saw Moses, and behold, the skin of his face shone, and they were afraid to come near him. (Exodus 34:29-30)

> (See Paul's commentary on this event: "The ministry of death, carved in letters on stone, came with such *glory* that the Israelites could not gaze at Moses' face because of its *glory*." 2 Corinthians 3:7, RSV)

> Like the appearance of the bow that is in the cloud on the day of rain, so was the appearance of the *brightness all around.* Such was the appearance of the likeness of *the glory of the LORD.* And when I saw it, I fell on my face, and I heard the voice of one speaking. (Ezekiel 1:28)

> And *the glory of the LORD* went up from the cherub to the threshold of the house, and the house was filled with the cloud, and the court was filled with *the brightness of the glory of the LORD.* (Ezekiel 10:4)

> And in the same region there were shepherds out in the field, keeping watch over their flock by night. And an angel of the Lord appeared to them, and *the glory of the Lord shone around them, and they were filled with great fear.* (Luke 2:8-9)

God revealed his presence to his people in other ways, as well: through a burning bush,[21] pillars of cloud and fire,[22] in lightning and thunder,[23] and within the cloud-enshrouded tabernacle.[24] They were tokens of God's presence, emblems of his dwelling and activity among mortals.[25] They, too, are his glory.

What about Divine Visitations in our day? Does God still manifest his presence in auras of light, or in pillars of cloud and fire? Is it possible that we might come upon a bush that burns with the presence of God? It is within his power if it suits his purpose. The God who is present with us in every moment and in every place (whether we know it or not) can make his presence known in visible and tangible ways. It is important for us to affirm this. I have never witnessed a tornado moving ominously across the sky, but knowing that others have and can tell me about these sky funnels increases my respect for the power at work in our world. Even if we never have the experience ourselves, we should live in a state of openness to glory in the event that God surprises us! It is important for us to know that he is such a God. We should keep ourselves in a posture of readiness to encounter God in his incandescent presence and be amazed.

THE GRAIL OF GLORY

If God reveals his presence in the world, then the greatest adventure we can know is the quest to discover his glory. Our grail is not the famed cup of Christ, hidden to mortals, but God himself, disclosed to all who seek him:

> You will seek the LORD your God and you will find him, if you search after him with all your heart and with all your soul. (Deuteronomy 4:29)
>
> I love those who love me, and those who seek me diligently find me. (Proverbs 8:17)
>
> You will seek me and find me, when you seek me with all your heart. (Jeremiah 29:13)
>
> And without faith it is impossible to please him, for whoever would draw near to God must believe that he exists and that he rewards those who seek him. (Hebrews 11:6)
>
> May all who seek you
> rejoice and be glad in you! (Psalm 40:16; 70:4)

Life at its best includes watching for God and his activity in our lives:

> O my Strength, I will watch for you,
> for you, O God, are my fortress.
> My God in his steadfast love will meet me. (Psalm 59:8-9)

We ought to live each day with the hope and expectation of meeting God in whatever ways he may reveal his presence to us.[26] It is important for us to factor this into our understanding of God; otherwise we are in danger of a faith that becomes a mere abstraction and has little to do with our lives in the world. That may be the creed of Deists, who believe that God does not act in the world he made, but it is not the God and Father of our Lord Jesus Christ.[27]

Watch for things that don't fit the normal pattern of your experience. Look for the extraordinary in the course of the ordinary. For the unusual in the midst of the usual. For something that stands out to you as uncommon in what would otherwise be a common setting. A Presence. A Voice. A Shimmering. A Movement. A Perturbation. A subtle Change in the currents of the world around you.[28] Our quest to encounter God in his glory requires discernment and results in delight: discerning signs of God's presence in our lives, and delighting in them; looking for tangible tokens of the Intangible One wherever he bestows them, and rejoicing in that revelation. "May all who seek you rejoice and be glad in you!"[29]

God promises that those who seek him with whole hearts will find him. He is pleased with those who do. He rewards those who do.[30] The reward for seeking God? Finding him! This is where the glory is. This is where our joy will be.

GOODNESS AND GLORY

When Moses asked God, "Show me your glory" the response to him was, "I will make all my goodness pass before you, and will proclaim before you the name, The LORD. . . ."[31] Sometimes glory is a disclosure of the goodness of God, his moral excellence, or moral beauty.[32] To say that God is beautiful in this way is to say that he is to our hearts what a rainbow or a sunset is to our senses. What color, form, and texture are to a work of art, the goodness of God is to the worshiping heart. To behold the beauty of the Lord is to experience him as the supremely desirable, delightful, and attractive.[33] As Jürgen Moltmann put it, "The beautiful in God is what makes us rejoice in him."[34] A.W. Tozer knew this same truth: "The blessed and inviting truth is that God is the most winsome of all beings, and in our worship of Him we should find unspeakable pleasure."[35] Do you know this beauty? Have you experienced this pleasure? It is glorious!

There is also the joy of discovering God's glory, or moral beauty, reflected in us. "And we all, with unveiled face, beholding the glory of the Lord, are being transformed into the same image from one degree of glory to another. For this comes from the Lord who is the Spirit."[36] We can't know the glory of God in life, enjoy his presence, delight in his beauty, and remain the same. A spiritual transformation takes place. His beauty gradually, by degree, becomes ours. Jonathan Edwards wrote:

> Another emanation of divine fulness, is the communication of virtue and *holiness* to the creature: this is a communication of God's holiness; so that hereby the creature partakes of God's own moral excellency; which is properly the beauty of the divine nature. And as God delights in his own beauty, he must necessarily delight in the creature's holiness; which is a conformity to and participation of it, as truly as a brightness of a jewel, held in the sun's beams, is a participation or derivation of the sun's brightness, though immensely less in degree.[37]

There is great joy here: an incredulous joy in becoming a stained-glass window through which God's glory shines, a surprised pleasure in becoming a tangible token of his presence in the world, a delight in being changed "from one degree of glory to another."[38]

A GREATER GLORY

If the apostle Paul is right (and I am confident that he is), there is greater glory in God's transformational work in us today than there was in the epic events that surrounded the giving of the law through Moses:

> Now if the ministry of death, carved in letters on stone, came with such *glory* that the Israelites could not gaze at Moses' face because of its *glory*, which was being brought to an end, will not the ministry of the Spirit have even more *glory*? For if there was *glory* in the ministry of condemnation, the ministry of righteousness must far exceed it in *glory*. . . . For if what was being brought to an end came with *glory*, much more will what is permanent have *glory*. . . . Now the Lord is the Spirit, and where the Spirit of the Lord is, there is freedom. And we all, with unveiled face, *beholding the glory of the Lord*, are being transformed into the same image *from one degree of glory to another*. For this comes from the Lord who is the Spirit. (2 Corinthians 3:7-18)

To know the presence and work of the Spirit is to know the glory of God. It may not seem as dramatic as the theophanies of the Old Testament, but it is not at all inferior. That we can think otherwise means only that we don't know what we are talking about. Paul saw the truth undimmed: The life-transforming presence and power of the Spirit is a greater glory than the extraordinary light that transformed the countenance of Moses.[39]

In this era of the Spirit, the glory of God in its most significant mode does not impinge upon our senses, but upon our hearts. But it is no less the glory of God for that! Paul was struck blind when his eyes beheld the glory of the risen Christ on the road to Damascus.[40] But he also claimed that all believers encounter the "glory of God in the face of Christ" shining in their hearts.[41] It is the same Christ and the same glory.

The earth is full of God's glory,[42] but so is our joy.[43] Joy betokens the presence of God no less than the beauty and wonders of nature,[44] or shafts of light appearing from no visible source. In the inner work of the Spirit we truly behold the glory of the Lord,[45] and in that gaze of the heart, we discover another dimension of our joy. This does not minimize the glory of God in the world; it exalts his glory in our hearts. The first is very great, the second even greater.

GOD'S GLORY IN CHRIST

If glory is a cut gem, God's glory in Christ is its largest and most lustrous facet. Jesus is the brightest and clearest of all the ways that God has made himself known. We find our greatest joy in him:

> Long ago, at many times and in many ways, God spoke to our fathers by the prophets, but in these last days he has spoken to us by his Son, whom he appointed the heir of all things, through whom also he created the world. *He is the radiance of the glory of God* and the exact imprint of his nature. (Hebrews 1:1-2)

> And the Word became flesh and dwelt among us, and *we have seen his glory, glory as of the only Son from the Father*, full of grace and truth. . . . No one has ever seen God; the only God, who is at the Father's side, he has made him known. (John 1:14, 18)

> The god of this world has blinded the minds of the unbelievers, to keep them from seeing the light of the gospel of *the glory of Christ, who is the image of God.* (2 Corinthians 4:4)

How do we connect with this glory when we have never seen Jesus? First, let me hold out to you the prospect that it is entirely possible, even in our day: "Though you have not seen him, you love him. Though you do not now see him, you believe in him and rejoice with joy that is inexpressible and filled with glory."[46]

There is a Gospel story about Jesus that we have come to know as "The Transfiguration." As soon as you read it you will recognize it as a story of glory:

> [Jesus] took Peter, John and James with him and went up onto a mountain to pray. As he was praying, the appearance of his face changed, and his clothes became as bright as a flash of lightning. Two men, Moses and Elijah, appeared in *glorious splendor*, talking with Jesus. They spoke about his departure, which he was about to bring to fulfillment at Jerusalem. Peter and his companions were very sleepy, but when they became fully awake, *they saw his glory* and the two men standing with him. As the men were leaving Jesus, Peter said to him, "Master, it is good for us to be here. Let us put up three shelters—one for you, one for Moses and one for Elijah." (He did not know what he was saying.) While he was speaking, a cloud appeared and covered them, and they were afraid as they entered the cloud. A voice came from the cloud, saying, "This is my Son, whom I have chosen; listen to him." (Luke 9:28-36, NIV)

This is a classic Divine Visitation: an incursion of the supernatural, a bright luminosity with no earthly source, a cloud, and an uncanny, otherworldly voice. I would have been frightened and bewildered, too!

But this is much more than classic. It is the Divine Visitation *par excellence*.[47] This glory eclipses the glory of all Visitations before it.[48] Glory envelopes Jesus, transforming his countenance with brilliant light. *Postmortem*, Moses and Elijah appear in "glorious splendor." And then God himself speaks from a cloud. Years later this event would be celebrated in these words:

> For we did not follow cleverly devised stories when we told you about the coming of our Lord Jesus Christ in power, but *we were eyewitnesses of his majesty*. He received honor and *glory* from God the Father when the voice came to him from *the Majestic Glory*, saying, "This is my Son, whom I love; with him I am well pleased." We ourselves heard this voice that came from heaven when we were with him on the sacred mountain. (2 Peter 1:16-18, NIV)

How do we come to know God's glory in his Son? By embracing what God says about him. As there were in the first century, there are many opinions about who Jesus is in our day.[49] But there is only one judgment that matters: God's, and he declares to us, "This is my Son." Here is the mystery and wonder of the Incarnation. In Jesus, God himself has come among us: "And the Word became flesh and dwelt among us, and *we have seen his glory, glory as of the only Son from the Father*, full of grace and truth."[50] This is where the glory is.

God's Word to us is not only that Jesus is his Son, but that he is chosen by God, beloved to God, the one in whom God delights. These are ways of describing the Messiah foretold by the prophets:

> Behold my servant, whom I uphold,
> my chosen, in whom my soul delights;
> I have put my Spirit upon him;
> he will bring forth justice to the nations. (Isaiah 42:1; compare Matthew 12:17-18)

To know God's glory in Christ, we must receive and affirm God's Word about him. He must be the Son of God *to us*, the Messiah *to us*, God's chosen and beloved *to us*, the one in whom *we* delight. And then, because he is all of this, we welcome God's word to us: "Listen to him." We cultivate a hunger and thirst for the words of Jesus. We treasure them above all other words. We believe his teaching. We obey his commands. We trust his promises. This is where the glory is. This is where we discover joy.

Questions for Thought and Discussion

1. What can you do to cultivate a sense of God's glory in the world? In what ways can you deepen and expand your joy in God's glory in the world?

2. If you know someone who venerates nature, and sees it as somehow divine, how would you go about introducing him or her to God's glory in nature, and how this is different and far greater?

3. Have you ever experienced a Divine Visitation? How would you describe your openness to that possibility in your life? What difference does this make to your understanding of God?

4. How can you put this Psalm into practice in your life? What would it look like?

> O my Strength, I will watch for you,
> for you, O God, are my fortress.
> My God in his steadfast love will meet me. (Psalm 59:8-9)

5. What are the implications of the Transfiguration for your understanding of Jesus? How does it affect your relationship with him?

CHAPTER 3

JOY AND GOD'S WORLD

Once upon a time, or before there was time, there was God, and only God. Then he created. He sang a pure and powerful song, and suddenly angels surrounded his throne. Myriads of heavenly creatures. Countless ranks. As they joined his song, lending harmony to the Maker's creative melody, galaxies and stars and planets, billions upon billions, came into existence.[1] And then his musical mandate brought forth a particular world, our own, filled with plants, insects, and animals – sea-swimmers, land-walkers, and sky-flyers – as many and varied as the luminaries in the night sky. Nearly finished, he sang once more and fashioned the crown of his handiwork, humans – a man and a woman – to mirror him in his world, and to steward and rule it in his stead.

Why did God create? The answer can't be that he was lonely or bored, that it was a whim or an inadvertence, that he was somehow compelled to do it, or that there was a deficit in his existence that could only be remedied by creating a universe. None of this can be true of the Supreme Being.[2] God's life was full and complete before he spoke the first word of creation. This is the right answer to our question: God created from the plenitude of his pleasure. He created from the overflow of his joy.[3] It was his pleasure to create; it is ours that he did.

God is not only joyful beyond imagination, he generous beyond words.[4] If we rejoice in him, we are also invited to enjoy his gifts. He welcomes us to delight in the things he has made – which makes our joy as high as the heavens and as wide as the world.

Joy is first and foremost our enjoyment of God, but he intends our joy to include the world he has made.[5] Pleasures of the earth are not meant to rival our joy in God, but to enlarge and enrich our experience of his goodness. He takes pleasure in what he has made, and invites us to do so as well:

> May the glory of the LORD endure forever;
> may the LORD rejoice in his works. (Psalm 104:31)

> At the works of your hands I sing for joy. (Psalm 92:4)

> Great are the works of the LORD, studied by all who delight in them. (Psalm 111:2)

> The godly, wheresoever they cast their eyes, beholding heaven and earth, the air and water, see and acknowledge all for God's wonders; and, full of astonishment and delight, laud the Creator, knowing that God is well pleased therewith.[6]

Creation expands the arena of our joy. It is meant to include not only our Maker, but his world. God intends our joy to be a celebration of his joy in his handiwork and the pleasure of being beneficiaries of his overflowing generosity.

THE EARTH IS FULL OF HIS GLORY!

The enjoyment of the world is more than the enjoyment of the world. It is an encounter with the One who made the world, is everywhere present in it, and reveals himself through it. If you delight in the beauty of a rainbow, you are not merely observing a refraction of light through moisture in the air; you are beholding the colorful glory of God. If you have ever huddled in your house as the night sky was ripped by bolts of lightning and thunder shook your bones, you witnessed more than an electrical storm; you came face to face with the raucous glory of God. If you've ever felt dwarfed as you walked through a rivered canyon, with peaks towering to the heavens around you, you experienced more than your smallness in a very big world; you were humbled by the immense glory of God.

There is more to the world than the world itself. In the words of Peter Kreeft, "There is something bigger than the world out there hiding behind everything in the world, and our chief joy is with it."[7] Our chief joy is with God himself, present in, and revealing himself through, all that we encounter in the world:

> Holy, holy, holy is the LORD of hosts;
> the whole earth is full of his glory. (Isaiah 6:3)

> Do I not fill heaven and earth? declares the LORD.
> (Jeremiah 23:24)

> The heavens declare the glory of God,
> and the sky above proclaims his handiwork.
> Day to day pours out speech,
> and night to night reveals knowledge.
> There is no speech, nor are there words,
> whose voice is not heard.
> Their voice goes out through all the earth,

> and their words to the end of the world. (Psalm 19:1-4)

> You should turn . . . to a living God who made the heaven and the earth and the sea and all that is in them. In past generations he allowed all the nations to walk in their own ways; yet he did not leave himself without witness, for he did good and by giving you from heaven rains and fruitful seasons, satisfying your hearts with food and gladness. (Acts 14:15-17)[8]

God is not another name for nature. He is not it. He is Other. That is his transcendence. He is neither identical to, nor bound by, his creation. Nevertheless, he fills it. He is everywhere present in it, from the inner life of an atom to the outer reaches of the farthest galaxies. Wherever you turn he is there, behind and before, on either side, above and below, and deep within.[9] His sovereign power and animating presence orders and sustains life in every moment and in every place. That is his immanence.[10]

The presence of God in creation is intangible, but the *tokens* of his presence are not. They are constantly presented to us as divine revelation. In fact we cannot escape them, even if are unaware of them.[11] They surround us at all times as his glory filling the earth, as the many and varied manifestations of the invisible, ubiquitous God. This includes the pleasures of the world. C.S. Lewis saw it truly: "I was learning the far more secret doctrine that *pleasures* are shafts of the glory as it strikes our sensibility. As it impinges on our will or our understanding, we give it different names – goodness or truth or the like. But its flash upon our senses and mood is pleasure."[12] Pleasure whispers the goodness of God to us.[13] It sings his love for us. It is a splash of his overflowing joy.

A WORLD FOR US

Why did God create? Because it was his joy to do so. Why did he create a world of beauty and fragrances and textures and sounds, and sentient creatures like us to inhabit it? For our joy. All the wonders and pleasures of creation are meant for us. Luther saw this truth clearly:

> Our loving Lord God will that we eat, drink, and be merry, making use of his creatures, *for therefore he created them.* He will not that we complain, as if he had not given sufficient, or that he could not maintain our poor carcasses; he asks only that we acknowledge him for our God, and thank him for his gifts.[14]

Calvin concurred: "The Lord himself, by the very order of creation, has demonstrated that he created all things *for the sake of man.*"[15] In our own day Nicholas Wolterstorff has written: "When the Christian affirms the goodness of the physical creation, he is not just praising its magnificence. He is saying that the physical creation is good *for human beings.* It serves human fulfillment."[16]

When we affirm the truths of creation, it is not enough to say that God created, or even that what he created is good. God created, all of his creation is good, and all of it is meant for us. The apostle Paul did not retreat from this startling notion:

> All things are yours . . . the world or life or death or the present or the future – all are yours. (1Corinthians 3:21-22).

> Everything created by God is good, and nothing is to be rejected if it is received with thanksgiving. (1 Timothy 4:4)

> [God] richly provides us with everything to enjoy. (1 Timothy 6:17)

This does not give us license to indulge selfish desires, but liberty to celebrate the goodness of God's world, and the rightness of our pleasure in it. It was given for our joy, and, through our thankful enjoyment of it, to reflect the beneficence of our God. Arthur Holmes was right: "If God's creation has value, then the enjoyment of its benefits can celebrate God's goodness. All of life, in fact, becomes just such a celebration – provided one recognizes the one who made it so heartily good."[17]

THE SACRED SECRET

C.S. Lewis wrote, God "likes matter. He invented it."[18] He created the heavens and the earth and then made corporeal beings to inhabit them. Of all the worlds he might have brought into being, he chose this one with all of its tangible properties.

Matter is God's invention, and pleasure is his gift. God created us not only to steward his world, but to savor it. The physical world, our senses, and minds that transcend and appreciate sentient experience point to something greater than themselves. They bear witness to the Creator's design for pleasure. There is something mysterious and wonderful here! Pleasures are "the faint, far-off results of those energies which God's creative rapture implanted in matter."[19] We seriously misunderstand matter and seriously mistake pleasure if we don't see them in relation to the Creator and his good and wise design for us.

Pleasure as we know it is not only sacred by virtue of its divine origin and blessing, it is a gift that is ours alone. In the words of Pascal, we are neither angels nor brutes.[20] Lacking bodies, angels are incapable of experiencing the sensory dimension of pleasure. Lacking our cognitive abilities, brutes are incapable of its appreciative dimension. Angels may know reflective delights, and animals, pleasurable stimuli, but only we can enjoy them both, and enjoy them in the same experience. It is unique to us. We profane our pleasures when we treat them as less than sacred. We diminish them when we do not delight in them as the "secret that . . . [God] has shared with us alone."[21]

CREATION, FALL, AND REDEMPTION

I can guess what you are thinking, and you are right. All of this sounds too Edenic. It doesn't reckon with the Fall and the effect of sin upon the world and our affections.[22] After all, the Bible says some pretty negative things about the pursuit of pleasure.[23] We can't simply affirm pleasure without qualification in our world. Augustine saw the problem clearly:

> Within also, within is another evil, arising out of the same kind of temptation; whereby they become empty who please themselves in themselves . . . . But in pleasing themselves, they much displease You, not merely taking pleasure in things not good, as if they were good, but in Your good things as though they were their own; or even as if in Yours, yet as though of their own merits; or even if as though of Your grace, yet not with friendly rejoicings . . . .[24]

Lewis saw this perversion of pleasure at the very heart of the Fall: "Someone or something whispered that they could become as gods – that they could cease directing their lives to their Creator and taking all their delights as uncovenanted mercies . . . which arose in the course of a life directed not to those delights but to the adoration of God."[25]

Does our sinful state make delight in the world's pleasures a bad thing? Some Christians have thought so. For them, pleasures that are unnecessary for personal survival or the continuation of the human race should be shunned. The few that are indispensable to those ends, like eating and procreation, are necessary evils, permitted as sparingly as possible, with a sense of embarrassment and even shame that we must make concessions to them.

I can't believe that this is what God intends for us! It is not the world, but worldliness, that is evil – treating the pleasures of the world as ends in themselves. It is not sensory experience, but sensualism, that is evil – treating pleasure as if it defined the meaning of our lives.

Good is so much more powerful than evil (because God is so much more powerful than his adversaries) that the fallenness of our world cannot negate the goodness of God's gifts to us in creation. Faced with ascetics in his day who urged abstinence from marriage and certain foods, the apostle Paul labeled their teaching "doctrines of demons," and "hypocrisy," and those who advocated it "liars seared in their own consciences as with a branding iron."[26] His antidote for such error? Affirming the goodness of God's creation even in a fallen world. The pleasures of marriage and food are good gifts "which God has created to be gratefully shared in by those who believe and know the truth. For everything created by God is good, and nothing is to be rejected, if it is received with gratitude: for it is sanctified by means of the word of God and prayer."[27]

C.S. Lewis wrote:

> But aren't there bad, unlawful pleasures? Certainly there are. But in calling them "bad pleasures" I take it we are using a kind of shorthand. We mean "pleasures" snatched by unlawful acts." It is the stealing of the apple that is bad, not the sweetness. The sweetness is still a beam from the glory. That does not palliate the stealing. It makes it worse. There is a sacrilege in the theft. We have abused a holy thing. . . .[28]

Sin has spoiled much that is good about pleasure, but this is an indictment of us, and not of pleasure itself. The gift is still good; our desecration of it is evil.

A Christian approach to pleasure will be shaped by the truths of Creation, Fall, and Redemption: meeting pleasure first with affirmation and celebration because all that God creates is good, then with a sober reckoning of sin and its ramifications, and finally with joyous reaffirmation, as the gifts of creation are reclaimed through the redemptive work of Christ and are restored to the Creator's good intentions for us.[29]

For some Christians, Redemption counters the Fall, but is irrelevant to Creation. Grace saves us from our sin, but has little to do with the heavens and the earth and our place in them. This is seriously incomplete, and seriously mistaken as a result! Redemption remedies the Fall and reclaims Creation. In fact, one day Creation will be raised to greater heights in the new heavens and the new earth, and the resurrection of our bodies.[30] The final state of the redeemed will not be an incorporeal mode of existence in a spirit-world, but glorified physical life in a newly created world whose wonders will far surpass those of Eden. The apostle Paul wrote of this:

> For the creation was subjected to futility, not willingly, but because of him who subjected it, in hope that the creation itself will be set free from its bondage to corruption and obtain the freedom of the glory of the children of God. For we know that the whole creation has been groaning together in the pains of childbirth until now. And not only the creation, but we ourselves who have the firstfruits of the Spirit, groan inwardly as we wait eagerly for adoption as sons, the redemption of our bodies. (Romans 8:20-23)

In the present, we must affirm the world, forsake it, and then enjoy it anew as a taste of God's goodness and a foretaste of the glories that await us in the new heavens and the new earth.[31]

PLEASURE AND THE RENEWING OF OUR MINDS

Our minds play an important role in our experience of pleasure.[32] Consider aesthetic pleasure. Augustine wrote: "There is no corporeal beauty, whether in the condition of a body, as figure, or in its movement, as in music, of which it is not *the mind* that judges."[33] According to Aquinas, "Beauty relates to the *cognitive* faculty."[34] Closer to our own day, David Elton Trueblood wrote, "In the appreciation of beauty the physical senses are involved, but they are by no means sufficient to the aesthetic result. Always there is a *process of thought.*"[35]

Not only do our minds assess properties like proportion, form, and unity, they make the summary judgment that something is beautiful, and invite our affections to respond in enjoyment. This is the truth behind the saying, "Beauty is in the eye of the beholder." Not so much in the eye as in the mind.

What is true of aesthetic pleasure is true, in nuanced ways, of all pleasures. They are never merely experienced, they are construed. In fact, the interpretation of a pleasure is integral to the pleasure itself. C.S. Lewis wrote:

> We can't – or I can't – hear the song of a bird simply as a sound. Its meaning or message ("That's a bird") comes with it inevitably – just as one can't see a familiar word in print as a merely visual pattern. The reading is as involuntary as the seeing. When the wind roars I don't just hear the roar; I "hear the wind." In the same way it is possible to "read" as well as to "have" a pleasure. Or not even "as well as." The distinction ought to become, and sometimes is, impossible; to receive it and to recognise its divine source are a single experience. This heavenly fruit is instantly redolent of the orchard where it grew. This sweet air whispers of the country from whence it blows. It is a message. We know we are being touched by a finger of that right hand at which there are pleasures for evermore. There need be no question of thanks or praise as a separate event, something done afterwards. To experience the tiny theophany is itself to adore.[36]

To *have* a pleasure and to *read* its divine Source ought to be, and can be, a single experience. The problem is that this doesn't happen automatically in our fallen state. For those in whom the Spirit of God is not at work, it doesn't seem to happen at all. They *have* the pleasure and *read* its significance apart from God. Pagan pleasure is a form of idolatry: It is wrongly construed, its Source is never honored, and the Giver is never thanked. It is sacrilege: stripping pleasure of its sacred dimensions and treating it as something profane.

If our pleasures are out of step with God's intention for them, whatever else may be the case, our thinking has gone wrong. When the apostle Paul indicted his generation for its perversion of pleasure, this is how he described the guilty parties:

> [They] suppress the truth.
> [They became] futile in their thinking.
> [Their] foolish hearts were darkened.
> Claiming to be wise, they became fools.
> [They] exchanged the truth about God for a lie.
> God gave them up to a debased mind.[37]

In our fallen state, there is perversion in our pleasures. Decadence in our delights. The dispositions of our hearts are bent. Our affections are disordered. Our thoughts are disoriented. That is the bad news. Here is the good news: This can be redeemed! Luther wrote:

> Nature, which is corrupted by original sin, is unable to enjoy without abuse the things created and given by God, not because this is the nature of created things but because the heart of him who uses them is evil. But if the heart has been reformed by the Spirit, it makes use of both the useful and the delightful things in a holy manner and with thanksgiving.[38]

Redemption brings about a radical change as we are "transformed by the renewing of our minds."[39] Pleasure is consecrated as truth is embraced, and the fruits of creation are received with thankful prayer. It is worth returning to the words of Paul: "God created [marriage and food] to be received with thanksgiving by those who believe and know the truth. For everything created by God is good, and nothing is to be rejected if it is received with thanksgiving, for it is made holy by the word of God and prayer."[40]

Here pleasure approaches its divine intention as a sign of God's presence in the world and a taste of his goodness. As our minds become habituated in a God-framed-and-centered-way-of-seeing-life, and we grow in conviction and confidence in this vision, not only do we find the sting removed from our hardships, we discover a greater joy in all that is positive and pleasurable in life.

It is important for us to affirm Creation and the Fall, acknowledging both the goodness of pleasure and our perversion of pleasure. Neither is the last word on the matter, however. The last word is Redemption, where the effects of the Fall are countered, and the bounty of Creation is consecrated and received as a token of God's goodness to us, and a sign that points our hearts to the wonders of the new heavens and earth that await us.

JOYFUL STEWARDS

If we look at the world through the lens of joy we will see God in all that we behold. In its vastness we will see his immensity. In its great antiquity we will see his eternal power. In its grandeur we will see his glory. In its wonders we will see his wisdom. In its intricacies we will see his genius. In its wildness we will see his sovereign freedom and surprising ways. In its pleasures we will see his goodness to us. If we see the world as it truly is, we will see it enchanted with the presence of God.[41]

If our first response to the world is anything but reverence, wonder, and awe, we haven't seen it truly. We are out of touch with reality. There is much that we will miss and much that we will misuse because we misunderstand the true nature and significance of the world. We will live in it like witless thugs throwing fine crystal into the air for target practice.

Our first calling as bearers of God's image is to enjoy and steward the earth as a theater for his glory.[42] We should do nothing to diminish it. Nothing to disgrace it. Nothing to sully it. Nothing to spoil it. We should do everything we can to protect it. Everything we can to preserve it. We should use but not abuse. We should enjoy but not exploit. Because it bears the presence of God, the earth is sacred. Because it is a habitation of God, it is holy. Our stewardship must begin here.

Our responsibility to steward the earth includes managing its resources for the good of humanity. God does not intend that some (who happen to have and control wealth) should enjoy the benefits of his world and others (who do not) should not. Nor does he intend that one generation should tap the resources of his world in a way that deprives future generations of them.[43] It isn't our planet. We don't have that right:

> The earth is the LORD's and the fullness thereof,
> the world and those who dwell therein. (Psalm 24:1)
>
> One generation shall laud your works to another,
> and shall declare your mighty acts. (Psalm 145:4)

It should come as no surprise that our stewardship of the earth is meant to reflect the two great commandments we have been given: to love God fully and supremely, and to love our neighbors as ourselves.[44] We are called to manage the resources of the world as an expression of love for its Maker and ours. We are called to steward its stores as an expression of love for our neighbor – near and far, present and future.

Now, our challenge as people who must live with their feet on the ground is how to pursue these things when so many care so little. What difference can we make when governments and corporations – power brokers who control, consume, and often contaminate the resources of the world – reject and even revile a true vision of God's world? Jesus would tell us that they must be included in our daily prayer:

> Our Father in heaven,
> hallowed be your name.
> Your kingdom come,
> your will be done,
>   on earth as it is in heaven. (Matthew 6:9-10)

The desecration and despoiling of God's world, and the unjust distribution of its resources, are spiritual problems. Until hearts are aligned with God's, and knees bow to his rightful dominion, there is little hope for a better world.

Whatever governments and private enterprises may say or do, there is a higher government to which we must answer, and a greater enterprise to which we have been enlisted. As far as it lies with us we should steward the earth for the glory of God and the good of others, and revel in the joy God gives as we do this. Then, to all who will listen, in our words and by our deeds, let us proclaim the truths of Creation and the joys of stewardship, and pray heartily that many more will join us!

Questions for Thought and Discussion

1. Daniel MaGuire has written, "Biblical joy is not a gossamer strain of otherworldly spirituality; it is of the earth and earthy." As you reflect on your view of joy before reading this chapter, would you characterize it as "otherworldly spirituality" or "of the earth and earthy"? Identify the factors that shaped your view.

2. How does God's joy in creation influence your view of the world?

3. Discuss the following quote from the chapter. Have you had similar experiences? How have they impacted your understanding of God?

> The enjoyment of the world is more than the enjoyment of the world. It is an encounter with the One who made the world, is everywhere present in it, and reveals himself through it. If you delight in the beauty of a rainbow, you are not merely observing a refraction of light through moisture in the air; you are beholding the colorful glory of God. If you have ever huddled in your house as the night sky was ripped by bolts of lightning and thunder shook your bones, you witnessed more than an electrical storm; you came face to face with the raucous glory of God. If you've ever felt dwarfed as you walked through a rivered canyon, with peaks towering to the heavens around you, you experienced more than your smallness in a very big world; you were humbled by the immense glory of God.

4. “Pleasure is consecrated as truth is embraced, and the fruits of creation are received with thankful prayer.” What would this look like as a daily practice for you?

5. How can you take the section “’Joyful Stewards” into conversations with your peers about environmental ethics and issues of global economics and justice?

CHAPTER 4

THE JOY OF SALVATION

If I could travel through history and visit any time and place in the world, after first century Palestine in the days of Jesus my destination would be the Garden of Eden before the human rebellion that took place there. Have you ever wondered why we are given no more than a tantalizing glimpse of Edenic life in the Sacred Word? I don't know the answer, of course. Perhaps God chose not to let us see more of that world because it would break our hearts and cripple our will to live in our own. Only he knows.

Sometimes my heart aches for Eden. For that ancient *garden of delights.*[1] I long for the world God first created. A world unspoiled and unsullied by sin. A world filled with tokens of the divine Presence, from the shimmering light of stars overhead to the cool, crystalline dew beneath one's feet at the dawning of the day, each and every one pointing vividly and irresistibly to its Source. I yearn for the world in which the knowledge of God was untrammeled, and every blink of the eye brought one into touch with some new dimension of his glory. I long for the day long past when no distinction was even possible between sensual and spiritual, when all pleasures were joyful, directed to God in thanksgiving and praise, and joy pulsed with pleasure in the Creator and the good world that he created.[2]

JOY LOST

Alas, that world did not survive. Perhaps it could not have. Its brevity is linked to the mystery of human freedom. The unthinkable happened. Our forebears chose the pleasure of the Creator's good gifts over the Creator himself. They chose to forge their own future rather than embrace the adventures God had in store for them. They chose to write their own story rather than play a part in God's. Though it was sheer folly to do so, they turned their will away from the will of God. The harmony between Being and being was destroyed. Real pleasures were lost, and sensual idols took their place. The joy that bound creature to creature and all created things to the Creator became a wistful memory. A whisper that few still hear, beckoning the heart to a better time and a better world.

Why did God make us free? Look at what we have done with our freedom! C.S. Lewis was right:

> God created things which had free will. That means creatures which can go either wrong or right. Some people think they can imagine a creature which was free but had no possibility of going wrong; I cannot. If a thing is free to be good it is also free to be bad. And free will is what has made evil possible. Why, then, did God give them free will? Because free will, though it makes evil possible, is also the only thing that makes possible any love or goodness or joy worth having. A world of automata – of creatures that worked like machines – would hardly be worth creating. *The happiness which God designs for His higher creatures is the happiness of being freely, voluntarily united to Him and to each other in an ecstasy of love and delight compared with which the most rapturous love between a man and a woman on this earth is mere milk and water. And for that they must be free.*[3]

Our freedom made joy possible. Our misuse of that gift shattered the fragile and precious jewel. Only shards remain, bits and pieces strewn over the sands of human experience like the remains of a long-lost and once-glorious civilization.

What great loss the Fall brought to our race!

We are used to living with our sin, like skunks at home with their own stench. We take as normal fare what the Bible treats as a great horror and scandal.[4] Nothing could be more abnormal than humanity in its fallen condition. Nothing more unnatural. In our sinful state we have exchanged the glory of God for smudgy little gods of our own making, and the wine of joy for the waste of our own perversions: an obscene draught, which, though it offends the sensibilities of heaven, we have come absurdly to prefer.

The Bible declares: "Those who choose another god multiply their sorrows."[5] To limit this to images of wood and stone is to miss the point. To make a god of anything other than the living and true God is to forsake the Fountain of Joy.[6] It is to drink instead from the fetid marshes of our own folly. Idols of the heart are not only tokens of defiance, but monuments to our insanity. The self-inflicted wounds of idolatry, in fact, are its greatest irony. Make a god of money and you will pierce your heart with many pangs.[7] Make a god of pleasure and you may as well try to grasp the wind in your hands.[8] Whatever our god, at whatever self-made shrine we bow, we forgo by that choice the joy for which we were created, and embrace a course that will lead only to sorrow beyond anything we can imagine. As Peter Kreeft put it, "Since an idol *is* not God, no matter how sincerely or passionately it is treated as God, it is bound to break the heart of the worshipper, sooner or later . . . . You can't get blood from a stone or divine joy from nondivine things."[9]

The temptation our first parents faced was to become like God.[10] They were enticed to leave their station under the gracious and sovereign rule of

God and to grasp at something they foolishly believed would be better. They sought a greater good; they found, instead, a Curse: alienation from the Creator, from themselves, from each other, and from all other creature-life. They made themselves petty deities, and, in that choice, multiplied their sorrow. Day after day brought forth new grief, from the painful memory of Eden-lost to the horrors of their own growing evil. It is an ancient story. Every chapter tells much the same tale. Only the times, places, and characters change. We are all sons of Adam and daughters of Eve. We have all shared in their sin and know their consequent sorrow.

This is the condition of fallen humanity. This is what it means to be "by nature children of wrath."[11] The wrath of God is not a bolt of lighting, thrown Zeus-like from the heavens to punish wrongdoers. *Wrath is joy rejected.*[12] Peter Kreeft is right: "But the opposite of true joy is far worse than anguish . . . . In fact, its opposite is hell."[13] Jesus' description of perdition is no pre-scientific fiction. It is as realistic as anything can be. Hell is a place of weeping and gnashing of teeth.[14] Ultimate sorrow and grief. If joy is found only in the undimmed presence of God,[15] and hell is the darkness of eternal separation from him,[16] there is no other way that it could be. Hell is the place of divine wrath: joy refused and forfeited with finality. It is the unending, unmitigated sorrow of choosing another god.[17] It became one of two destinies the day our first parents took their first steps from the Garden.[18]

JOY REGAINED

Fallen earth is neither Eden nor hell. Sin accounts for the first, and grace for the second. Short of hell, joy lost can be regained. In fact, this is the heart of our redemption.

The joy of God in salvation. The joy of salvation begins with the joy of the Savior.[19] Our joy, here, as everywhere, is sourced in the overflowing joy of God. His mercy is not meager, his goodness never grudging. It is lavish.

Profuse. A cascading waterfall. A coursing river. A fathomless, brimming well. A thirst-quenching drink poured into the dry and desolate hearts of men and women in desperate need of spiritual refreshment.[20]

Why did God become one of us in Jesus of Nazareth? The Nicene Creed answers this with the words, "For us human beings and for our salvation."[21] Our sin and misery created the need for God's action in Christ. But there is another question we can ask: Why would God do this?[22] Our need did not create an obligation for him. He could have left us in our sin and been fully just in doing so. Why did he not only script the drama of salvation, but in Christ step onto the stage of human history as its central character? Because it was his joy to do so.

With a sense of wonder the prophet Micah asked, "Who is a God like you, pardoning iniquity and passing over transgression?" No one! This is astonishing! Not at all what sinners should expect from a holy God! But there is an even greater wonder when we ask why God would deal with us so. Micah's answer takes us to the heart of God: "because he delights in steadfast love."[23] There is unimaginable pleasure here that only God can know. This insight into God's heart leapt to life in the assuring words of Jesus: "Fear not, little flock, for it is the Father's good pleasure to give you the kingdom."[24] And, "Just so, I tell you there is . . . joy in heaven over one sinner who repents" (a joy pictured in the parable with music, dancing and a great feast).[25]

The author of Hebrews wrote of Jesus: "For the joy that was set before him [he] endured the cross, despising the shame, and is seated at the right hand of the throne of God."[26] This joy was not merely the anticipation of future glory and his exaltation at the right hand of the Father. It was the joy of "bringing many children to glory," passing through death to "destroy the one who has the power of death, that is, the devil," and to "free those who all their lives were held in slavery by the fear of death."[27] It was the vision of his redemptive work completed in us and for us that brought him such joy, even in the hour of his greatest suffering and pain. So great was Christ's joy in bringing salvation to a sinful world that even the agony of the Cross was compelled to yield to it. If we cannot fathom his passion (and we cannot), we will never plumb his greater pleasure in its outcome. Nevertheless, our joy in salvation begins here. Our boon in redemption lies in the bountiful joy of our Redeemer.

Our joy in salvation. God enjoys bringing salvation to sinners, and sinners to salvation. It is a joy for him to renovate our hearts, opening them to all he has done for us, all that he is now doing, and all that he has pledged to do.[28] This transformation begins with the birth of something radically new within us. Jesus described it as being born again, born from above, born of the Spirit.[29] The apostle Paul put it in these words: "Therefore, if any one is in Christ, he is a new creation; the old has passed away, behold, the new has come."[30] This conversion from death to life is not something we do or could possibly bring about. It is the work of God, revolutionizing our innermost being and freeing us to live from a transformed heart. It is the genesis of our joy. A.W. Tozer wrote, "The very moment that the Spirit of God has quickened us to His life in regeneration, our whole being senses its kinship to God and leaps up in joyous recognition."[31] Our initiation into the joy of salvation lies here.

When grace triumphs in us, we come to revel in our need for God. Our plight brings us pleasure.[32] We experience grace as a feast offered to poor, famished, thirsty wayfarers a step away from perishing in their desperate want:

> Ho everyone who thirsts,
> come to the waters;
> and you that have no money,
> come, buy and eat!

> Come, buy wine and milk
> without money and without price.
> Why do you spend your money for that which is not bread,
> and your labor for that which does not satisfy?
> Listen carefully to me, and eat what is good,
> and delight yourselves in rich food.
> Incline your ear, and come to me;
> listen so that you may live. (Isaiah 55:1-3, NRSV)

In our sin we are utterly lost and ruined, without hope because we fully deserve the trouble we are in and can do nothing to change it. Nothing to escape it. We cannot see a light, and could not move toward it even if we did. Sin brings only unrelenting darkness and despair. And then. And then God. And then God transforms our troubled lot. He pardons us! Rescues us! Delivers us! He reaches down to us when we could not reach up to him. He meets us in our misery. He sings to us, sings over us, and puts his song within us. We are enchanted by the music. He washes away the filth that caked us. Mends our brokenness. Dresses and heals our wounds. Clothes our nakedness in robes that befit royalty. Fills our aching and empty souls. Quenches our terrible thirst. Then, to our utter amazement, he invites us into an "ecstasy of love and delight," C.S. Lewis wrote, "compared with which the most rapturous love between a man and a woman on this earth is mere milk and water."[33] Hands that covered our face in shame now lift in grateful praise, and we join Mary's song: "My soul magnifies the Lord, and my spirit rejoices in God my Savior!"[34]

The joy of salvation is a restoration of joy in the Triune God. It is not the kind of joy we experience in viewing a sunset or a meadow of alpine flowers. It is more like the gaiety of a wedding dance: delighting in one's beloved and the celebration of love and life together. The joy of salvation is a participation in God's joy: the Father's joy in the Son and the Spirit, the Son's joy in the Father and the Spirit, the Spirit's joy in the Father and the Son, and the shared joy of the Three-in-One. Sin destroyed the communion of joy our kind once shared with this Three-Personal God.[35] Redemption restores it. We are brought back to, and drawn into, this Fellowship, or Dance, of joy. Joy is then experienced in its highest and purest form as love's delight: joy in God's Triune love for us, our small, growing love offered back to the Father, Son, and Holy Spirit, and the love and joy we share with all who have entered into the life of God.[36]

Eschatological joy. Joy is not only a memory of what our race once knew (a dormant memory waiting to be awakened), it is a foretaste of what we will one day know without measure or end. Words falter in our attempt to describe it. Jonathan Edwards saw this joy as "exceeding great and vigorous; impressing the heart with the most lively sensation of inexpressible sweetness, mightily moving, animating, and engaging . . . [us] *like a flame of fire.*"[37] C.S. Lewis described it differently:

> We are to be re-made. . . . [We shall discover what] we have never yet imagined: a real Man, an ageless god, a son of God, strong, radiant, wise, beautiful, and *drenched in joy.*[38]

> The faint far-off results of those energies which God's creative rapture implanted in matter when He made the worlds are what we now call physical pleasures; and even thus filtered, they are too much for our present management. What would it be to taste at the fountain-head that stream of which even these lower reaches prove so intoxicating? Yet that, I believe, is what lies before us. The whole man is to drink joy from the fountain of joy. As St. Augustine said, the rapture of the saved soul will "flow over" into the glorified body. In the light of our present specialized and depraved appetites we cannot imagine this *torrens voluptatus* [*river of pleasure*], and I warn everyone most seriously not to try.[39]

Is the joy of heaven a flaming fire or a river of pleasure? Will it warm us or drench us? We should not be surprised that the best Christian minds use conflicting metaphors to describe it. If our present joy can be "inexpressible and full of glory,"[40] human language is pressed beyond its limits to describe the joy that will far surpass anything we have yet experienced. (When Lewis warned us against trying to imagine it, he was seeking to spare us headache and heartache!)

The joy that awaits the people of God is not entirely future. Nor am I saying only that hoping for this future bliss strengthens our joy in the present.[41] I am saying, and truly mean it, that a dimension of our present joy is the joy of the age to come breaking back into human history in advance of its final consummation. It is ours now in an experience that is *partial, prospective,* and given to us in a *paradox.*

Our experience of this eschatological joy is *partial.* It is a "taste" of the "powers of the age to come."[42] The feast is future, but our taste of it in the present is no less real for that. The fruit of our present joy grows in the same orchard as heaven's joy. Jonathan Edwards wrote: "The love and joy of the saints on earth is the beginning and dawning of the light, life, and blessedness of heaven, and is like their love and joy there; or rather, the same in nature, though not the same in degree and circumstance."[43] Joy is one. Our experience may be partial, but joy itself cannot be parsed.

We still await the full and perfect realization of the Spirit's work, transforming our bodies and souls and fitting them for life in the age to come with its new heavens and new earth.[44] In the present, however, he is given to us as "the guarantee of our inheritance until we acquire possession of it."[45] We have received the first installment! It is not only a promise of what is still future to us, it is a realization of it in part. The Spirit's presence in our lives now is the "first fruits" of the full harvest that will come at the end of days.[46] It is a brand of fire from the blazing joy of the age to come. A splash from the river of pleasure in which we will one day be drenched.

Our experience of the joy of salvation is not only partial, it is *prospective.* By its very nature it anticipates. It points to the future, where it truly belongs and where it will be fully known.[47] The joy of salvation brings to us a poignant sense of being an alien in this fallen world, a misfit, a stranger, a pilgrim. The experience is both a presence and an absence of joy: The joy present delights our hearts, but the joy absent (because it is still future to us) creates a longing so powerful that it nearly breaks them. Its taste sharpens a hunger that will be fulfilled in what the Seer called the Marriage Feast of the Lamb:

> Let us rejoice and exult
> and give him the glory,
> for the marriage of the Lamb has come,
> and his Bride has made herself ready. (Revelation 19:7)
>
> Happy are those who are invited to the wedding supper of the Lamb. (Revelation 19:9)

Those who know this joy "desire a better country, that is, a heavenly one."[48] Their hearts yearn for their true homeland: the "city of God," with angels beyond count in "festal gathering."[49] They are both blessed and bereft until joy's consummation in the coming Kingdom.

Finally, the joy of salvation is given to us in a *paradox*, created by the fact that it is a taste of the "powers of the age to come"[50] while we still live in "the present evil age."[51] We are caught between two ages. We live "between the times," as George Eldon Ladd put it.[52] We are people who must daily embrace the dialectic of "already" and "not yet," of being "sorrowful, yet always rejoicing."[53] We experience something of the joy of the age to come even in the travail of this age. Peter captured this paradox as well as anyone:

> Blessed be the God and Father of our Lord Jesus Christ! By his great mercy we have been born anew to a living hope through the resurrection of Jesus Christ from the dead, and to an inheritance which is imperishable, undefiled, and unfading, kept in heaven for you, who by God's power are guarded through faith for a salvation ready to be revealed in the last time. In this you rejoice, though now for a little while you may have to suffer various trials." (1 Peter 1:3-6).

Both sides of the paradox must be affirmed and embraced. This age, in a death rattle, lingers; in Christ the age to come has broken back into the present in advance of its final consummation, bringing, in a preliminary way, the blessings and benefits of the "salvation ready to be revealed in the last time." Christian living is thus characterized by suffering (which belongs to this age) and the new birth (which belongs to the age to come). It is distinguished by a living hope and an undaunted joy in the face of life's worst.

The joy of salvation is anchored in the death and resurrection of Christ. His death belongs to this present evil age, and is, in fact, its most heinous crime.[54] His resurrection belongs to the age to come. It is the "first fruits" of a harvest that is still future.[55] In Christ the two ages have met, like two titans in combat, or, more accurately, like an invading force (the age to come) arriving to conquer an evil empire (this age). The enemy has not yet drawn his last breath, and in fact still seeks to wreak havoc wherever he can. In Luther's words, "His rage we can endure, for *lo, his doom is sure*!"[56] To be "in Christ," to use Paul's characteristic way of describing our status in redemption, is to live in one age, but to be a citizen of another. It is to live in evil's domain, but to belong to the rightful, conquering King. It is to suffer the gasping wrath of a dying regime, and at the same time be confident in our Champion's ultimate conquest. It is to be kept by his protective power, and to face the stiffest tests of life with the indomitable joy that only he can give.

Cosmic joy. Finally, as we think about the consummation of God's redemptive plan in the new heavens and the new earth, we must bring passages like these into our hope:

> Let the heavens be glad, and let the earth rejoice;
> let the sea roar, and all that fills it;
> let the field exult, and everything in it!
> Then shall all the trees of the wood sing for joy
> before the LORD, for he comes . . . . (Psalm 96:11-12)
>
> Let the sea roar, and all that fills it;
> the world and those who dwell in it!
> Let the floods clap their hands;
> let the hills sing for joy together
> before the LORD, for he comes . . . . (Psalm 98:7-8)
>
> For you shall go out in joy,
> and be led forth in peace;
> the mountains and the hills before you
> shall break forth into singing,
> and all the trees of the field shall clap their hands . . . .
> (Isaiah 55:12)

Those of us who would feel at home in Lewis' Narnia or Tolkien's Middle Earth can imagine an animated nature rejoicing in its Maker. Is this how we are to take these passages? Will we behold this with the eyes of our glorified bodies in the new heavens and new earth? I hope so! But it is at least true that these cameos of redeemed nature are meant to tell us that a total environment of joy is the ideal for all created life, and that one day this will be realized.[57] Martin Luther wrote that in the resurrection people will "play with heaven and earth, the sun and all the creatures." And "All creatures shall have their fun, love and joy and shall laugh with thee and thou with them . . . ."[58] When the ancient harmony of Eden is restored, and raised to even greater heights, all creatures – in ways suited to their creaturehood – will reflect the glory of the Creator, and will, in that mirrored glory, know the creature's share in the shared joy of the Father, Son and Holy Spirit. A flaming fire. A river of pleasure.[59]

Questions for Thought and Discussion

1. How does our culture deny or diminish the seriousness of sin? Why is it important for us to come to grips with the bad news about our human condition before we can appreciate the good news of what God has done for us in Christ?

2. "Those who choose another god multiply their sorrows." (Psalm 16:4) How has this played out in your own life? The lives of people you know? Our culture? What are the gods of this generation?

3. Why is God's joy in our salvation important? Why is it important to see "joy regained" as the centerpiece of redemption? What difference does it make? What difference does it make to the way you talk with unbelieving friends about the Gospel?

4. Why is it important to link our present joy to the future joy of the Kingdom? What difference does this make to your experiences of joy?

5. How do you see the paradox of already-not-yet in your life and your experience? Why is it important to affirm both sides of the paradox? What implications are there if we only affirm one or the other?

Chapter 5

Joy and the Word of God, Part 1

"Oh! How great and glorious a thing it is to have before one the Word of God! With that we may at all times feel joyous and secure."[1] Martin Luther wrote the words, but many have known this joy. Long before Luther, sacred poets reveled in the same pleasure:

> In the way of your testimonies I delight
> as much as in all riches. (Psalm 119:14)
>
> I find my delight in your commandments,
> which I love. (Psalm 119:47)
>
> Oh how I love your law!
> It is my meditation all the day. (Psalm 119:97)
>
> How sweet are your words to my taste,
> sweeter than honey to my mouth! (Psalm 119:103)
>
> Your testimonies are my heritage forever,
> for they are the joy of my heart.[2] (Psalm 119:111)

Delighting in God's written Word to us is a high peak in the mountain range of joy. As we explore it we will begin on a broad path at its base, and then wind our way upward, narrowing our course as we approach its spectacular summit.

JOY AND OUR VISION OF LIFE

If you are like many, you separate the rational and emotional dimensions of our human nature. Theologians sometimes distinguish between "faculties" of the soul, such as intellect, emotion, and will.[3] Maybe you aren't that theoretical. Still, you may think that reason and emotions belong in different categories. They aren't the same kind of thing. Emotions seem like reflexes: they happen to us in an involuntary sort of way. Reason, on the other hand, is deliberate and intentional. Emotions are a spontaneous, and reason a studied, way of interacting with the world.

Actually, emotions are more complex than they seem when we experience them. They are rooted in our thought life. This is so because emotions are interpretive in nature. We don't delight in things unless we *perceive* them as something to be desired. We don't fear things unless we *regard* them as something that could be dangerous to us. We don't become angry with someone unless we *construe* their actions to be contrary to our expectations or desires. We don't grieve the loss of someone or something unless we *see* ourselves bereft of something we value.[4] Without this interpretive dimension (an activity of our minds) we would not have emotions as we know them. Robert Roberts puts it this way: "Human life, even when it is far from intellectual, is fundamentally a life of the mind."[5] In every emotion there is an act of interpretation, even if it happens so quickly and unobtrusively that we are unaware of it.

Let's see where this path takes us. Our interpretations of life never hang mid-air. They don't take place in isolation, ad hoc, or on their own. They are part of a larger web of beliefs we have about the world and our place in it. This is another way of talking about a worldview. A worldview is the lens through which we see the world and our life in it. It is the orientation of our hearts that gives us our bearings as we journey through life. It is the larger narrative framework in which we understand our story. Although we can and should think about our worldview, and think and reason from it, more often than not it operates tacitly, beneath the surface of our awareness. In the experience of an emotion we may not notice it at all. Nevertheless, it is always there, helping us make sense of life.[6] Worldviews are essential to emotions as we experience them.[7] Whether you've ever given a thought to it or not, you have one and it is crucial to your prospects for joy.[8]

Paul Holmer wrote: "Christian beliefs are like the river-bed for one's thoughts and emotions, within which contentment, peace and joy can truly flourish."[9] If you turn to the pages of Scripture, you will discover the same truth:

> Not only that, but we *rejoice* in our sufferings, *knowing that* suffering produces character . . . . (Romans 5:3)
>
> You *joyfully* accepted the plundering of your property, *since you knew* that you yourselves had a better possession and an abiding one. (Hebrews 10:34)
>
> *Count it all joy*, my brothers, when you meet trials of various kinds, *for you know* that the testing of your faith produces steadfastness. (James 1:2-3)

The sacred authors share a belief that joy flourishes in a vision of life in which our hearts are shaped and informed by the knowledge of God and his ways.[10]

JOY AND ITS REASONS

Josef Pieper wrote, "Man can (and wants to) rejoice only when there is a reason for joy. And this reason, therefore, is primary, the joy itself secondary."[11] We enjoy God *because* we believe that he is our Creator and Redeemer. We enjoy the world *because* we believe it to be the amazing work of our amazing God. We rejoice in our circumstances *because* we see them as the work of a sovereign Lord for our good. We rejoice in our salvation *because* we regard it as the highest and best gift that could ever be given to us in our plight. These are the reasons for joy. Take them away, or prove them false, and joy would disappear with them.[12]

Where do we learn the truths that are essential to joy? Where do we learn the reasons for joy? From God, as he has made himself known to us through prophetic voices, supremely through his Son, our Lord Jesus Christ, and through the witness of the apostles – all vouchsafed to us in the Sacred Scriptures.[13] The path to joy leads us here:

> Long ago, at many times and in many ways, God spoke to our fathers by the prophets, but in these last days he has spoken to us by his Son, whom he appointed the heir of all things, through whom also he created the world. (Hebrews 1:1)

> For whatever was written in former days was written for our instruction, that through endurance and through the encouragement of the Scriptures we might have hope. (Romans 15:4)

> You have known the Holy Scriptures, which are able to make you wise for salvation through faith in Christ Jesus. All Scripture is God-breathed and is useful for teaching, rebuking, correcting and training in righteousness, so that the servant of God may be thoroughly equipped for every good work. (2 Timothy 3:15-16, NIV)

> "Man shall not live by bread alone, but by every word that comes from the mouth of God." (Matthew 4:4)

Paul wrote to the church in Rome: "May the God of hope fill you with all joy and peace *in believing.*"[14] Joy is God's gift to those who believe, to those who affirm that his Word to us is true.[15] This is not optional for joy. It is the only environment in which joy can flourish and grow. The Scriptures give us the truths that are essential for joy. They give us the reasons for joy, which we embrace in a life of faith. (Declining biblical literacy among those who profess faith in Christ, and the loss of joy in our generation, are linked, ball and chain. A Bible on the shelf is powerless to bring joy!)

JOY AND THE DISCOVERY OF TRUTH

Have you ever wondered why the discovery of truth is exhilarating?[16] Why did Archimedes jump from his bathtub and run naked into the street, crying "Eureka!" when he realized how to prove that the king's golden crown was a fraud? Why do we respond with an "Aha!" when the moment of discovery comes, instead of meeting it with a yawn? Why is there an irrepressible impulse to tell others? Why is it nearly impossible – whatever the field of knowledge – to keep the news to oneself? Because there is delight in discovery. Truth unveiled occasions joy as beauty evokes aesthetic pleasure, and a good joke brings laughter. Why is this so? Why do we find joy in the discovery of truth? This is how Augustine would have answered the question: "For a happy life is joy in the truth. For this is joy in You, who are the truth."[17] Underline the other side of this colon: Our joy in discovering truth is always, and never less than, a connection with the God of all truth.[18]

Whether we know it or not, it is the encounter with God in every discovery of truth that brings joy. C.S. Lewis pictured truth as a shaft of divine glory striking our minds.[19] To change the metaphor, all truth wafts the fragrance of its Homeland. Joy is our pleasure in its heavenly bouquet. We do not create truth. We can only discover it.[20] It is given to us. It is revealed. Disclosed. However it comes to us, whatever its mode of reception, all truth is from God. It is the encounter with him that brings us joy.

If all truth is God's truth, we may enjoy it wherever it is discovered.[21] Augustine wrote: "All good and true Christians should understand that truth, wherever they may find it, belongs to their Lord."[22] Calvin had the same vision of life:

> Not a particle of light, or wisdom, or justice, or power, or rectitude, or genuine truth, will anywhere be found, which does not flow from him, and which he is not the cause; in this way we must learn to expect and ask all things from him, and thankfully ascribe to him whatever we receive.[23]

> In reading profane authors, the admirable light of truth displayed in them should remind us, that the human mind, however much fallen and perverted from its original integrity, is still adorned and invested with admirable gifts from its Creator. If we reflect that the Spirit of God is the only fountain of truth, we will be careful, as we would avoid offering insult to him, not to reject or condemn truth wherever it appears. In despising the gifts, we insult the Giver.[24]

Enjoying his gifts glorifies the Giver.

To discover truth in nature is to touch the garment of God. To find it in our humanity is to see his reflection. To learn it in history is to trace the fingers of his sovereign hand. To encounter truth in Scripture, however, is to hear his beckoning voice and behold the beauty of his countenance. Here is one of our greatest joys! Calvin was right:

> Now this power which is peculiar to Scripture is clear from the fact that of human writings, however artfully polished, there is none

> capable of affecting us at all comparably. Read Demosthenes or Cicero; read Plato, Aristotle, and others of that tribe. They will, I admit, allure you, delight you, move you, enrapture you in wonderful measure. But betake yourself from them to this sacred reading. Then, in spite of yourself, so deeply will it affect you, so penetrate your heart, so fix itself in your very marrow, that compared with its deep impression, such vigor as the orators and philosophers have will nearly vanish. Consequently, it is easy to see that the Sacred Scriptures, which so far surpass all gifts and graces of human endeavor, breathe something divine."[25]

This is what we mean when we call the Bible the "inspired Word of God." It is God-breathed.[26] It is the product of his creative breath. It breathes truth *from* God *about* God and his ways. There is no truth nobler than this. No truth loftier or more sublime. And so it is that there is no joy-in-truth greater than joy in God's Word.

JOY AND THE GOD OF THE WORD

Joy in the Word of God is always at the same time joy in the God of the Word. This is so because biblical revelation, by its very nature, is both personal and propositional.[27] The inspired Word is both a coming of God and communication from God. It conveys the presence of God and truth about God and his ways. It is both event and word, relational and intelligible, self-disclosing and informative.

It is important for us to speak of both dimensions of biblical revelation because the written Word is the Word of the living God. The Spirit who inspired the Word continues to speak through the Word. What he once communicated through the pen of sacred scribes he speaks today through the same written Word. Stephen spoke of "living oracles" given to future generations through Moses.[28] Peter wrote of the "living and abiding word of God."[29] And the writer of Hebrews added:

> For the word of God is living and active, sharper than any two-edged sword, piercing to the division of soul and of spirit, of joints and of marrow, and discerning the thoughts and intentions of the heart. And no creature is hidden from his sight, but all are naked and exposed to the eyes of him to whom we must give account. (Hebrews 4:12-13)

The Bible is the living Word of the living God. In it the breath of God is dynamically present. In Calvin's words again, "the Sacred Scriptures, which so far surpass all gifts and graces of human endeavor, breathe something divine." In his conversion from atheism, Emille Cailliet, former professor of Princeton Theological Seminary, discovered that the pages of the Bible are "animated by the Presence of the Living God and the Power of His mighty acts."[30] In the entire world there is no other literature like this!

We wander from the path if we separate the Word of God and the Spirit of God in our understanding of the Bible. In the words of Donald Bloesch, "The word that proceeds from the mouth of God is filled with the power of the Spirit, bringing life and renewal to those dead in sin. . . . The Word derives its efficacy from the Spirit and the Spirit teaches what he has already disclosed in the word of Scripture." [31] The practical import of this union of the Word and the Spirit is that joy in God's Word is always at the same time joy in the God of the Word. It is joy in the truth given in Scripture, and joy in the Truth-giver whose presence is known and whose voice is heard in the written Word.[32]

THE JOYS OF MEDITATION

Joy can come to us through reading the Scriptures, or hearing them recited, preached, or sung. It comes most powerfully, because it engages our inner life most fully, in meditation. When we reflect deeply on the Word of God, the joys that we have explored in this chapter converge in a single point.[33]

Joy and our vision of life. Let's retrace some of our steps. Joy, like all emotions, is interpretive in nature. It is perspectival. It flourishes and is most robust in a God-centered vision of life that is formed and informed by his Word. Now, how does this become ours in a way that results in joy? What takes the Word of God into the deep currents of our hearts where our understanding of life is formed and our way of living is shaped? What sinks the Word into our innermost being where God delights to see truth at work?[34] Meditation.

To understand why this is so, we can use Jonathan Edwards' distinction between two kinds of knowing: "There is a distinction to be made between a mere *notional understanding*, wherein the mind only beholds things in the exercise of a speculative faculty; and *the sense of the heart,* wherein the mind not only speculates and beholds, but *relishes* and *feels*."[35]

A cursory reading of the Bible yields a *notional understanding* of what is written. An understanding of words and ideas. Some people never get beyond this in their knowledge of the Scriptures. It is in meditation, in the sacred interface between the Spirit-inspired Word and a Spirit-filled heart, when the lines between reflection, worship, and prayer become blurred and even insignificant, that the deep affections of our hearts are engaged and transformed by truth. It is this *sense of the heart* – the aim of meditation - that creates the conditions for joy.

A *notional understanding* of God and his ways will change nothing about us. A *sense of the heart* can change everything. In sensing and savoring truth – the heart of meditation – we are transformed by it. It touches our formative values: the things we treasure and hold dear at the most profound level of who we are. It changes our interests and concerns, our hopes and fears, our dreams and aspirations. It transforms what we think about and how we think about it.[36] It forges new ways of understanding the world, and creates a new vision of life.

Joy and the discovery of truth. Meditation embraces a paradox: Truth is both disclosed and discovered. It is revealed, but we must open ourselves to the revelation. It comes to us, but we must pursue it. And we must pursue it with passion:

> Yes, if you cry out for insight
> and raise your voice for understanding;
> if you seek it like silver
> and search for it as for hidden treasures;
> then you will understand the fear of the LORD
> and find the knowledge of God.
> For the LORD gives wisdom;
> from his mouth come knowledge and understanding. (Proverbs 2:3-6, RSV)

Meditation does not create a Zen-like void within. It creates a heart filled with thoughts of God. It is not cool, detached reflection. It is white hot, ablaze with a desire to know God and his ways. It is involved, invested, intent, and even intense. It is never mere observation. It is more like an obsession!

These are the essential features of meditation: disclosure, discovery, and delight. God discloses truth to us; we discover what he has disclosed; when disclosure and discovery meet, we experience great delight. Hearts devoted to God and his Word enjoy truth not as information but as illumination. Not merely as proposition, but as pleasure. God's Word becomes honey to our hearts, and a feast to our souls:

> How sweet are your words to my taste, sweeter than honey to my mouth! (Psalm 119:103)

> Your words were found, and I ate them, and your words became to me a joy and the delight of my heart (Jeremiah 15:16).

Joy and the God of the Word. I promised you a majestic summit when we began our climb. Here it is: The joy of meditation reaches its peak in the enjoyment of God who speaks through his Word. This joy begins with the cry of our hearts, "Beyond the sacred page, we seek thee, Lord!"[37] It is fulfilled as the sacred Presence is mediated through the sacred Page. It is not just a knowing, but a meeting. An encounter. At its highest and best, meditation is reflecting on the Word of God in the presence of God. As one Old Testament scholar put it, "The heart of meditation is the sheer enjoyment of the presence of the living Lord."[38] It is seeking communion with God in his Word, as the Spirit who once inspired the Word now creates a spiritual fellowship through the Word. If you have experienced this joy, accepting anything less would be like running a race but stopping short of the finish line, like ending a climb at a lower peak when the summit and its breath-taking vistas are within reach, like settling for an appetizer when the entrée is still to come:

> My soul is feasted as with a rich feast,
>   and my mouth praises you with joyful lips,
> when I think of you on my bed,
> and meditate on you in the watches of the night.
> (Psalm 63:5-6, NRSV)

The enjoyment of God in his Word is a consummate pleasure, as the truth of God illumines our minds, the will of God captivates our wills, the splash of his presence refreshes our hearts, the sound of his voice beckons us, and the beauty of his perfections holds us spellbound. Nothing will center your life, focus your heart, strengthen your resolve, assure you of truth, and encourage you in a God-pleasing life more than an encounter with the Living Lord through the Living Word.

Questions for Thought and Discussion

1. What difference does it make to understand that your emotional life and your thought life are interrelated?

2. What difference is there between these two statements, and how would you respond to someone who affirms the second, but not the first?

   "All truth is God's truth."
   "Everything is true."

3. What implications are there for seeing all truth as a connection with the God of truth?

4. How does it help you to make a distinction between a "notional understanding" and a "sense of the heart" in the way you approach the Scriptures? How have these two kinds of knowledge played out in your Christian life?

5. Describe your experience with meditation. How does it compare with the discussion of meditation in this chapter? Have you been inspired or encouraged to make changes? If so, in what ways?

Chapter 6

Joy and the Word of God, Part 2

We should give thanks for the men and women whose scholarship helps us understand the Bible, and take advantage of their work if we can. We should also be thankful, however, that we don't need to be scholars to read the Bible in ways that bring us into an encounter with God and a heart-shaping, thought-directing, life-changing, relationship with him.[1] An open Bible and an open heart are all that is necessary for joy.

Lectio Divina

As you study the Scriptures, let me recommend an ancient practice to you: *lectio divina*.[2] It is a way of interacting with the Word of God for the sake of communing with God.[3] It includes four movements of the heart: *lectio* (reading), *meditatio* (meditating), *oratio* (praying) and *contemplatio* (contemplating).[4]

Lectio. In the ancient world not many could read, and even fewer possessed copies of the Scriptures. For most people the reading of the Word was an auditory event: listening to someone read to them. Jewish people gathered in synagogues to hear the Scriptures read. Early Christians did the same when they assembled and their leaders fulfilled the apostolic injunction: "Devote yourself to the public reading of Scripture."[5]

Let this shape your *lectio*, or reading of the Scriptures. Think of reading as listening. Picture yourself in the synagogue in Nazareth, listening to Jesus read the Sacred Word to you:

> And he came to Nazareth, where he had been brought up. And as was his custom, he went to the synagogue on the Sabbath day, and he stood up to read. And the scroll of the prophet Isaiah was given to him. He unrolled the scroll and found the place where it was written,
>
> "The Spirit of the Lord is upon me,
> because he has anointed me
> to proclaim good news to the poor.
> He has sent me to proclaim liberty to the captives
> and recovering of sight to the blind,
> to set at liberty those who are oppressed,
> to proclaim the year of the Lord's favor."
>
> And he rolled up the scroll and gave it back to the attendant and sat down. And the eyes of all in the synagogue were fixed on him. And he began to say to them, "Today this Scripture has been fulfilled in your hearing." And all spoke well of him and marveled at the gracious words that were coming from his mouth. (Luke 4:16-22)

Or imagine yourself in this setting with Jesus and two disciples after the resurrection:

> That very day two of them were going to a village named Emmaus, about seven miles from Jerusalem, and they were talking with each other about all these things that had happened. While they were

> talking and discussing together, Jesus himself drew near and went with them. . . . And he said to them, "O foolish ones, and slow of heart to believe all that the prophets have spoken! Was it not necessary that the Christ should suffer these things and enter into his glory?" And beginning with Moses and all the Prophets, he interpreted to them in all the Scriptures the things concerning himself. (Luke 24:13-27)

In the discipline of *lectio* we read, eager to be addressed. We read, longing to hear the word of Christ. We read, picturing Christ himself reading to us, opening the Scriptures to us. We read, listening with rapt attention to him.

The reading involved in *lectio* should not only engage your mind, but your imagination and your affections. Bring yourself wholly to the Sacred Word, and allow it to address every dimension of who you are. Just as God spoke in "many and various ways" to our ancient family of faith,[6] so he does to us today.[7] He may address your mind with truth that illumines the path of life. His Word to you may strike your imagination with vivid pictures that enable you to *see* truth for your life. He may speak to your hopes and fears, your longing for love, your cry for peace, your yearning for significance, your desire for joy. *Lectio* seeks and is open to all of this.

As you read the Scriptures in a daily regimen for spiritual health, take note of passages and verses that capture your attention, and come back to them in your *lectio*. Read your chosen text at least twice. Many recommend reading aloud. The first time through, read without stopping. Then read it again slowly, attentively, and expectantly, with your mind alert and your heart open to possibilities: "Read the text selected at least once aloud, and then repeat it more slowly until you are stopped by a word or phrase that speaks to you. Listen for the word that seems to shimmer, beckon, unnerve, or challenge you. You are listening for God's voice in the sacred text."[8]

Meditatio. You are now ready for the second movement in *lectio divina*: Meditation. Reading the Scriptures whets your spiritual appetite; in meditation you eat your fill and enjoy. Reading the Word gives you a taste; in meditation you relish and delight. Reading gives you the lay of the land; in meditation you walk a path, linger along the way, stop, and sit for a while to appreciate and enjoy your surroundings.

When he was faced with temptation, Jesus quoted the ancient Scripture, "Man shall not live by bread alone, but by every word that proceeds from the mouth of God."[9] The Word of God is spiritual food. It feeds and nourishes us in our life with God. Sadly, we've become too accustomed to "fast food" and "eating on the run" to appreciate this metaphor. Meditation is a meal in which we sit, take our time, eat slowly, ruminate (literally, "chew"), and savor as we are filled.[10]

In your *meditatio*, focus on a word or phrase that arrested your attention in your reading. Stay here. There is only one Voice you want to hear. Put a finger to your lips and hush all others. Clear your mind of every distraction. Picture every diversion walking out of the room, leaving you quiet before God, in a position to give him your full attention. Be purposeful. Focus. Affirm God's presence with you.

Read the text again and again. Repetition is essential to meditation. Let it become a rhythm. Reflect on the sacred words and pay attention to the thoughts that come to you. Explore them. Let them lead you into new terrain. If images come to your mind, let them come clearly into view. How do they illumine what you've read? How do they relate to you and your life with God? Lower the guard you have set around your emotions, and open your heart to ways in which God may wish to speak to this important dimension of who you are. Let his Word bring sorrow, grief, conviction, joy, delight, hope, thankfulness, wonder, awe, or courage. Trust God with your vulnerability in this moment. Thank him for his loving, careful touch. Give freedom to your emotions and embrace them as part of God's communication with you. Be prepared to laugh or to weep!

Oratio.[11] Prayer isn't something we add to our reading and meditation. It is the Godward focus of all that we are doing. We approach our reading of the Scripture prayerfully, asking God to meet with us, to guide and direct us, to speak to us. We set aside any agenda that we may have, and come to the Scriptures with the prayer, "Not my will but yours be done."[12] As we move into meditation, prayer is an inner attentiveness. An openness and readiness to hear God's voice, and to see whatever he may show us. It is the invitation, "Speak, LORD, for your servant in listening."[13]

Oratio is also a distinct movement in *lectio divina.* Begin by incorporating your chosen text into a prayer. Let its words become yours, offered back to God. Personalize them with your own name. Rewrite them with "I" "me," "my." If they are *about* God, translate them into language addressed *to* God. If inspiration comes, sing them to God. He is your only audience, and he welcomes your musical offering! If the words of the text don't lend themselves to a prayer, hold the open Scriptures upward to God, and let the lifting up of your hands be your prayer.[14]

As you interact with a sacred text in meditation you will find yourself touched, stirred, and invited to respond. Whatever your response, wrap it in prayer and present it to God. It may be a prayer of longing and desire. It may be a prayer of worship and wonder. It may be a prayer of thanksgiving. Maybe it will be a prayer of confession and sorrow. You may find yourself striving with God, wrestling with challenges and questions in your life. You may be stirred to implore God to act in some way in your life or in the world around you. God may bring others to your mind and you will pray for them. It may be prayer without words, because you simply can't find them.[15] It may be a listening prayer as you wait before God to hear his voice. It may be a thankful recognition of God's presence with you.

Contemplatio. The word *contemplation* is a visual term.[16] It involves looking at something with steady focus and continued attention. We might contemplate the vastness of the universe, or the beauty and wonders of the world. It is a way of seeing things in a certain way as a result of careful and continuous observation. In our context, contemplation involves directing the "eyes of our hearts" to God,[17] and then envisioning the world through the Scriptures – which reveal God's vision of the world to us, filtered through the limitations of our humanity.[18]

Reading, meditating, and praying the Scriptures will bring a new perspective on life. We see God, the world, ourselves, and others in ways that we otherwise would not. We see things in light of who God is, what he has done, what he is doing, and what he has pledged to do. The apostle Paul wrote to the church in Corinth, "For the love of Christ controls us, because we have concluded this: that one has died for all, therefore all have died; and he died for all, that those who live might no longer live for themselves but for him who for their sake died and was raised."[19] Contemplate this long and clearly enough, and you will see yourself and others in a different way: "From now on, therefore, we regard no one according to the flesh. Even though we once regarded Christ according to the flesh, we regard him thus no longer. Therefore, if anyone is in Christ, he is a new creation. The old has passed away; behold, the new has come."[20]

This leads us to a second way in which we use the word "contemplation." It involves imagining possibilities in ways that lead us to act in ways that we otherwise would not. For instance, a young couple might contemplate marriage. They imagine what it would be like. They see themselves in that covenant relationship. They picture its potential. They envision its possibilities. Doing this results in decisions they make and a path they take. Or a couple might contemplate retirement from the work force. They imagine what life might look like if they were to take that action, they put themselves in imagined life scenarios, and then they make decisions and set a course for themselves as a result.

When the apostle Paul contemplated the love of Christ and his sacrificial death and resurrection, he saw people in a new and different way. This in turn led him to envision the world in a new light, to see new possibilities, to see himself in those possibilities, and to embrace a course of action to which God was calling him:

> All this is from God, who through Christ reconciled us to himself and gave us the ministry of reconciliation; that is, in Christ God was reconciling the world to himself, not counting their trespasses against them, and entrusting to us the message of reconciliation. Therefore, we are ambassadors for Christ, God making his appeal through us. We implore you on behalf of Christ, be reconciled to God. (2 Corinthians 5:18-20)

Contemplatio envisions bold new possibilities for our world and places us squarely in the mix. It brings a new awareness of the world as God sees it, and then activates and energizes us to participate with him in what he is doing. We become agents of redemption. In Christ, through us, God reconciles the world to himself. This is amazing. Truly amazing!

Make the disciplines of *lectio divina* a way of life. Make them a way of living in the Word and by the Word. There is formative power here that will change you. There is a fullness and fruitfulness in life that can only be found here. There is an intimacy with God that you can only enjoy here. There are pleasures of the heart that only those who walk this path can know:

> In the way of your testimonies I delight
> as much as in all riches. (Psalm 119:14)

Joy and the Word of God, Part 2

I find my delight in your commandments,
which I love. (Psalm 119:47)

Oh how I love your law!
It is my meditation all the day. (Psalm 119:97)

How sweet are your words to my taste,
sweeter than honey to my mouth! (Psalm 119:103)

Your testimonies are my heritage forever,
for they are the joy of my heart. (Psalm 119:111)

Questions For Thought and Discussion

1. Spend time in the Scriptures every day for a week, using the interactive questions found in Endnote 2 of this chapter. How did this change your time in the Word? How did this play out in your life in ways that caught your attention?

2. How does reading-as-listening change your approach to the Scriptures? Is it helpful to imagine Christ reading the Word to you, and listening to him? If you did this, describe your experience.

3. After implementing the discussion of *meditatio* in this chapter, describe how it engaged your imagination and emotions in ways that were meaningful to you.

4. As you reflect on your practice of *lectio divina* in the last week, what part did prayer play? In what ways were you led to pray in response to your meditation?

5. As you practice *lectio divina,* how do you see your vision of life changing? How do you see yourself changing to become part of this new perspective? In what ways do you sense yourself being summoned to be part of what God is doing?

ABOUT THE AUTHOR

In 1983 Rick and Sue Howe moved to Boulder, Colorado, where they raised three children – Amberle, Lorien, and Jamison – and have devoted more than thirty years to campus ministry at the University of Colorado. In addition to writing and speaking, Rick now leads University Ministries, whose mission is to "inspire and nurture a thoughtful pursuit of Christ, one student, one professor, one university at a time." To learn more about Rick, visit his website at www.rickhowe.org. You can also follow him on Facebook at *Rick Howe on Joy* and on Twitter @rickhoweonjoy. To learn more about University Ministries, see www.university-ministries.org.

ENDNOTES

PREFACE

1 Proverbs 17:22

2 Dallas Willard, *Renovation of the Heart: Putting on the Character of Christ* (Colorado Springs, CO: NavPress, 2002), p. 133.

3 Peter Kreeft, *Heaven: The Heart's Deepest Longing* (San Francisco: Ignatius Press, Expanded Edition, 1980), p. 129.

CHAPTER 1: THE GREATEST OF ALL PLEASURES

1 See "The Highest and Best of All Pleasures" in Rick Howe, *Path of Life: Finding the Joy You've Always Longed For* (Boulder, CO: University Ministries Press, 2017)).

2 "With you is the fountain of life; in your light do we see light." (Psalm 36:9, NRSV)

3 Aquinas wrote: "When they desire any good whatsoever, whether by intellective, sensitive, or unconscious appetite, all things desire God as their end, for nothing attracts but for some likeness to God." *St. Thomas Aquinas: Philosophical Texts*, ed. and trans. Thomas Gilby (Durham, North Carolina: The Labyrinth Press, 1982), p. 130.

4 Augustine wrote, "But when you enjoy a human being in God, you are really enjoying God rather than the human being. You will be enjoying the one, after all, in whom you find your bliss." Saint Augustine, "Teaching Christianity" in *The Works of Saint Augustine: A Translation for the 21st Century*, trans. Edmund Hill (Hyde Park, NY: New City Press, 1996), p. 122.

5 Whether it is traced to its Source or not, we enjoy the "fragrance of the knowledge of Christ." See 2 Corinthians 2:14 – "But thanks be to God, who in Christ always leads us in triumphal procession, and through us spreads the fragrance of the knowledge of him everywhere."

6 If you read *Path of Life*, you may remember these words from Chapter 4, "The Joy of the Lord."

7 Augustine, "The Confessions," in *Basic Writings of Saint Augustine* , ed., Whitney J. Oates (Grand Rapids: Baker Book House, 1980), Vol. I, p. 3. I have modernized the English translation.

8 Pascal, *Pascal's Pensées*, trans. W.F. Trotter (New York: E.P. Dutton & Co., Inc., 1958), p. 113.

9 "*Delight yourself in the LORD*, and he will give you the desires of your heart." (Psalm 37:4)

10 Jonathan Edwards wrote: "[True saints] first rejoice in God as glorious and excellent in himself, and then secondarily rejoice in it, that so glorious a God is theirs." Jonathan Edwards, "On Religious Affections," *The Works of Jonathan Edwards,* Perry Miller, Gen. ed., (New Haven: Yale University Press, 1959), Vol. 2, pp. 249-50.

11 Augustine wrote, of God, "Thou art an everlasting joy to Thyself!" St. Augustine, "Confessions," in *The Basic Writings of Saint Augustine,* ed., Whitney J. Oates (Grand Rapids: Baker Book House, 1948, repr. 1980), p. 114. According to Aquinas, God "possesses joy in Himself and all things else for His delight." And, "God is happiness by His Essence: for He is happy not by acquisition or participation of something else, but by His Essence." Aquinas, *Summa Theologica,* trans. Fathers of the English Dominican

Province (London: Burns Oates & Washburn, Ltd., third ed. 1941), I, Q. 26, A. 1., and I, II, Q. 3., A. 1.

For a development of this theme, see "The Joy of the Lord" in Howe, *Path of Life.*

12 Edwards wrote, "The first foundation of the delight a true saint has in God, is his own perfection; and the first foundation of the delight he has in Christ, is his beauty; he appears in himself the chief among ten thousand, and altogether lovely." Jonathan Edwards, "On Religious Affections," pp. 249-50.

13 Ibid.

14 Bruce Demarest quotes Morton Kelsey: "In Protestantism, God became a theological idea known by inference rather than a reality known by experience." He then adds: "Through a 'left-brain' approach to the faith, God easily becomes an abstraction removed from lived experience. A.W. Tozer noted that even as many scientists lose God in His world . . . so many theologians lose God in His Word." Bruce Demarest, *Satisfy Your Soul* (Colorado Springs: NavPress, 1999), p. 96.

15 See:

> In the year that King Uzziah died, I saw the LORD sitting on a throne, high and lofty; and the hem of his robe filled the temple. Seraphs were in attendance above him; each had six wings: with two they covered their faces, and with two they covered their feet, and with two they flew. And one called to another and said:
>
> "Holy, holy, holy is the LORD of hosts;
> the whole earth is full of his glory."
>
> The pivots on the thresholds shook at the voices of those who called, and the house filled with smoke. And I said: "Woe is me! I am lost, for I am a man of unclean lips, and I live among a people of unclean lips; yet my eyes have seen the King, the LORD of hosts!" (Isaiah 6:1-5, NRSV)

16 Psalm 34:8, RSV

17 For the larger context of this hymn, see the verses before and after:

> For just as you were at one time disobedient to God but now have received mercy because of their disobedience, so they too have now been disobedient in order that by the mercy shown to you they also may now receive mercy. For God has consigned all to disobedience, that he may have mercy on all. (Romans 11:31-32)
>
> I appeal to you therefore, brothers, by the mercies of God, to present your bodies as a living sacrifice, holy and acceptable to God, which is your spiritual worship. (Romans 12:1)

18 "And before him no creature is hidden, but all are open and laid bare to the eyes of him with whom we have to do." (Hebrews 4:13, RSV).

19 Psalm 90:14, NRSV

The experience of God was so vivid to hearts that poets used the language of perception to describe it. For example:

> As for me, I shall behold your face in righteousness;
> when I awake, I shall be satisfied with your likeness. (Psalm 17:15)
>
> My eyes are ever toward the LORD. (Psalm 25:15)
>
> Your steadfast love is before my eyes. (Psalm 26:3)
>
> One thing have I asked of the LORD,
> that will I seek after:
> that I may dwell in the house of the LORD
> all the days of my life,
> to gaze upon the beauty of the LORD
> and to inquire in his temple. (Psalm 27:4)

20 See also:

> Who is a God like you, pardoning iniquity
> and passing over transgression
> for the remnant of his inheritance?
> He does not retain his anger forever,
> because *he delights in steadfast love.* (Micah 7:18)
>
> I praise You, O Father, Lord of heaven and earth, that You have hidden these things from the wise and intelligent and have revealed them to infants. Yes, Father, for this way was *well-pleasing in Your sight.* (Luke 10:21, NASB)
>
> Fear not, little flock, for it is your Father's *good pleasure* to give you the kingdom. (Luke 12:32)

21 I explore the sorrow of God in "The Joy of the Lord" in *Path of Life.* In brief, God's joy is found in who he is and what he does; his sorrow is a response to who we have become, and what we do, in our sin.

22 Dallas Willard, *The Divine Conspiracy: Rediscovering Our Hidden Life in God* (Harper Collins Publishers: San Francisco, 1998), p. 61.

23 John 15:11

24 This is what the apostle Paul meant, I think, when he said that we "have the mind of Christ." (1 Corinthians 2:16). It is thinking about things the way Christ would.

25 Mark 9:24.

26 Theologians make a distinction between the "ontological" Trinity and the "economic" Trinity. The ontological Trinity refers to God as he exists in himself. It is who God is. The economic Trinity refers to what this God does, and how he makes himself known in the world and the affairs of human beings (The word "economic" is from the Greek *oikonomikos,* signifying the arrangement of activities and affairs in a household.) My

explanation of the how the Trinity came to be known and understood among early followers of Jesus falls under the rubric of the economic Trinity. This is not the old error of modalism, which says that the Father, Son, and Holy Spirit, are three modes in which the one God reveals himself. God reveals himself as a Trinity because he is a Trinity.

27 When Jewish people were asked who their God was, they told the stories of Abraham, Isaac and Jacob, and the God who was revealed to their ancient forefathers. When Christians were asked what deity they worshiped, they, too told a story: "Ours is the God of Israel, who has now made himself known uniquely and consummately in Jesus the Messiah, and in the Spirit poured out upon our Messianic community." They found their own story, and their understanding and experience of God, in this Story. It was not a theological dissertation. (The term *Trinitas* did not come into being until the early third century.) It was a tale that leapt to life in their encounter with God.

28 For example:

> Pray then like this:
> 'Our Father in heaven,
> hallowed be your name.' (Matthew 6:9)

29 Although it was not a major theme in his teaching or in the Jewish Scriptures which shaped his teaching, Jesus used feminine images (but not feminine titles) for God. These, too, connect with our experience of God. In the trilogy of parables about something lost and found (a sheep, a coin, a son) in Luke 15, the one who seeks what is lost represents God: a shepherd, a woman, and a father. When he spoke the following words, he drew from the Old Testament tradition of likening God's parental love for his people to mothers in the animal world:

> O Jerusalem, Jerusalem, the city that kills the prophets and stones those who are sent to it! How often would I have gathered your children together as a hen gathers her brood under her wings, and you were not willing! (Matthew 23:37)

For its Old Testament background, see:

> He [God] found him [Israel] in a desert land,
> and in the howling waste of the wilderness;
> he encircled him, he cared for him,
> he kept him as the apple of his eye.
> Like an eagle that stirs up its nest,
> that flutters over its young,
> spreading out its wings, catching them,
> bearing them on its pinions,
> the LORD alone guided him,
> no foreign god was with him. (Deuteronomy 32:10-12)

> The LORD repay you for what you have done, and a full reward be given you by the LORD, the God of Israel, under whose wings you have come to take refuge!" (Ruth 2:12)

Keep me as the apple of your eye;
hide me in the shadow of your wings. (Psalm 17:8)

Be merciful to me, O God, be merciful to me,
for in you my soul takes refuge;
in the shadow of your wings I will take refuge,
till the storms of destruction pass by. (Psalm 57:1)

But I am the LORD your God
from the land of Egypt;
you know no God but me,
and besides me there is no savior.
It was I who knew you in the wilderness,
in the land of drought;
but when they had grazed,
they became full,
they were filled, and their heart was lifted up;
therefore they forgot me.
So I am to them like a lion;
like a leopard I will lurk beside the way.
I will fall upon them like a bear robbed of her cubs;
I will tear open their breast,
and there I will devour them like a lion,
as a wild beast would rip them open. (Hosea 13:4-8)

God is also pictured as a human mother:

For a long time I have held my peace;
I have kept still and restrained myself;
now I will cry out like a woman in labor;
I will gasp and pant. (Isaiah 42:14)

Can a woman forget her nursing child,
that she should have no compassion on the son of her womb?
Even these may forget,
yet I will not forget you. (Isaiah 49:15)

As one whom his mother comforts,
so I will comfort you;
you shall be comforted in Jerusalem. (Isaiah 66:13)

30 I understand that much of the language of "sonship" with respect to Jesus has to do with his role as Messiah. But Jesus himself used it in ways that went beyond that. See, e.g., Matthew 11:26-28 and Luke 10:21-23, and the sonship of Jesus throughout the Gospel of John.

31 John 15:11. See also John 17:13, NRSV: "But now I am coming to you; and I speak these things in the world, so that they may have my joy made complete in themselves."

32 Peter Kreeft, *Heaven: The Heart's Deepest Longing* (San Francisco: Ignatius Press, Expanded Edition, 1980), p. 159.

33 It put them into a state of "cognitive dissonance," as contemporary psychologists might describe it.

34 See the following:

> He committed no sin, neither was deceit found in his mouth. (1 Peter 2:22)
>
> For our sake he made him to be sin who knew no sin, so that in him we might become the righteousness of God. (2 Corinthians 5:21)
>
> You know that he appeared in order to take away sins, and in him there is no sin. (1 John 3:5)

35 "And they went into Capernaum, and immediately on the Sabbath he entered the synagogue and was teaching. And they were astonished at his teaching, for he taught them as one who had authority, and not as the scribes." (Mark 1:21-22)

36 See:

> And when he returned to after some days, it was reported that he was at home. And many were gathered together, so that there was no more room, not even at the door. And he was preaching the word to them. And they came, bringing to him a paralytic carried by four men. And when they could not get near him because of the crowd, they removed the roof above him, and when they had made an opening, they let down the bed on which the paralytic lay. And when Jesus saw their faith, he said to the paralytic, 'Son, your sins are forgiven.' Now some of the scribes were sitting there, questioning in their hearts, 'Why does this man speak like that? He is blaspheming! Who can forgive sins but God alone?' And immediately Jesus, perceiving in his spirit that they thus questioned within themselves, said to them, 'Why do you question these things in your hearts? Which is easier, to say to the paralytic, 'Your sins are forgiven,' or to say, 'Rise, take up your bed and walk'? But that you may know that the Son of Man has authority on earth to forgive sins'— he said to the paralytic— 'I say to you, rise, pick up your bed, and go home.'" (Mark 2: 1-11)

37 See, for example:

> All things have been handed over to me by my Father, and no one knows the Son except the Father, and no one knows the Father except the Son and anyone to whom the Son chooses to reveal him. (Matthew 11:27)
> I and the Father are one. (John 10:30)
>
> Do you not believe that I am in the Father and the Father is in me? The words that I say to you I do not speak on my own authority, but the Father who dwells in me does his works. Believe me that I am in the Father and the Father is in me, or else believe on account of the works themselves. (John 14:10-11)
>
> Jesus said to her, 'Do not cling to me, for I have not yet ascended to the Father; but go to my brothers and say to them, 'I am ascending to my Father and your Father, to my God and your God.' (John 20:17)

38 See, for example:

> One Sabbath he was going through the grainfields, and as they made their way, his

disciples began to pluck heads of grain. And the Pharisees were saying to him, 'Look, why are they doing what is not lawful on the Sabbath?' And he said to them, 'Have you never read what David did, when he was in need and was hungry, he and those who were with him: how he entered the house of God, in the time of Abiathar the high priest, and ate the bread of the Presence, which it is not lawful for any but the priests to eat, and also gave it to those who were with him?' And he said to them, 'The Sabbath was made for man, not man for the Sabbath. So the Son of Man is lord even of the Sabbath.' (Mark 2:23-28)

39 See the following:

> Not everyone who says to me, "Lord, Lord," will enter the kingdom of heaven, but the one who does the will of my Father who is in heaven. On that day many will say to me, "Lord, Lord, did we not prophesy in your name, and cast out demons in your name, and do many mighty works in your name?" And then will I declare to them, "I never knew you; depart from me, you workers of lawlessness." (Matthew 7:21-23)
>
> When the Son of Man comes in his glory, and all the angels with him, then he will sit on his glorious throne. Before him will be gathered all the nations, and he will separate people one from another as a shepherd separates the sheep from the goats. And he will place the sheep on his right, but the goats on the left. Then the King will say to those on his right, "Come, you who are blessed by my Father, inherit the kingdom prepared for you from the foundation of the world. For I was hungry and you gave me food, I was thirsty and you gave me drink, I was a stranger and you welcomed me, I was naked and you clothed me, I was sick and you visited me, I was in prison and you came to me." Then the righteous will answer him, saying, "Lord, when did we see you hungry and feed you, or thirsty and give you drink? And when did we see you a stranger and welcome you, or naked and clothe you? And when did we see you sick or in prison and visit you?" And the King will answer them, "Truly, I say to you, as you did it to one of the least of these my brothers, you did it to me." (Matthew 25:31-37)

40 C.S. Lewis famously wrote:

> I am trying here to prevent anyone saying the really foolish thing that people often say about Him: I'm ready to accept Jesus as a great moral teacher, but I don't accept his claim to be God. That is the one thing we must not say. A man who was merely a man and said the sort of things Jesus said would not be a great moral teacher. He would either be a lunatic – on the level with the man who says he is a poached egg – or else he would be the Devil of Hell. You must make your choice. Either this man was, and is, the Son of God, or else a madman or something worse. You can shut him up for a fool, you can spit at him and kill him as a demon or you can fall at his feet and call him Lord and God, but let us not come with any patronizing nonsense about his being a great human teacher. He has not left that open to us. He did not intend to.

C.S. Lewis, *Mere Christianity* (New York: Macmillan, 1952), pp. 55-56. For a recent defense of this argument, see David A. Horner, "*Aut Deus aut Malus Homo:* A Defense of C.S. Lewis's 'Shocking Alternative,' in *C.S. Lewis as Philosopher: Truth, Goodness and Beauty*, eds., David Baggett, Gary R. Habermas and Jerry L. Walls (Downers Grove, IL: InterVarsity Press, 2008).

41 If it hadn't been revealed to them, they could never have guessed it or reasoned their way to it:

At that time Jesus declared, "I thank you, Father, Lord of heaven and earth, that you have hidden these things from the wise and understanding and revealed them to little children; yes, Father, for such was your gracious will. All things have been handed over to me by my Father, and no one knows the Son except the Father, and no one knows the Father except the Son and anyone to whom the Son chooses to reveal him. (Matthew 11:25-27)

42 See:

When the day of Pentecost arrived, they were all together in one place. And suddenly there came from heaven a sound like a mighty rushing wind, and it filled the entire house where they were sitting. And divided tongues as of fire appeared to them and rested on each one of them. And they were all filled with the Holy Spirit and began to speak in other tongues as the Spirit gave them utterance. (Acts 2:1-4)

43 "And I will ask the Father, and he will give you another Helper, to be with you forever, even the Spirit of truth, whom the world cannot receive, because it neither sees him nor knows him. You know him, for he dwells with you and will be in you." (John 14:16-17)

44 Compare these passages:

And I will ask the Father, and he will give you another Helper, to be with you forever, even the Spirit of truth, whom the world cannot receive, because it neither sees him nor knows him. You know him, for *he dwells with you and will be in you.* (John 14:16-17)

I will not leave you as orphans; *I* will come to you. (John 14:18)

Now *the Lord is the Spirit,* and where the Spirit of the Lord is, there is freedom. And we all, with unveiled face, beholding the glory of the Lord, are being transformed into the same image from one degree of glory to another. For this comes from the Lord who is the Spirit." (2 Corinthians 3:17-18)

For what we proclaim is not ourselves, but Jesus Christ as *Lord,* with ourselves as your servants for Jesus' sake. (2 Corinthians 4:5)

Luke T. Johnson writes, "This Holy Spirit is not an impersonal force; it is the life-giving presence of the risen Lord." Luke T. Johnson, *The New Testament Writings: An Interpretation* (Philadelphia: Fortress Press, 1986), p. 107.

45 "But others mocking said, 'They are filled with new wine.'" (Acts 2:13)

46 "But you will receive power when the Holy Spirit has come upon you, and you will be my witnesses in Jerusalem and in all Judea and Samaria, and to the end of the earth." (Acts 1:8)

47 "And behold, I am sending the promise of my Father upon you. But stay in the city until you are clothed with power from on high." (Luke 24:49)

[48] See:

> And I will ask the Father, and he will give you another Helper, to be with you forever, even the Spirit of truth, whom the world cannot receive, because it neither sees him nor knows him. You know him, for he dwells with you and will be in you. "I will not leave you as orphans; I will come to you. . . . But the Helper, the Holy Spirit, whom the Father will send in my name, he will teach you all things and bring to your remembrance all that I have said to you. (John 14:16-18, 26)

[49] See the following:

> These things I have spoken to you while I am still with you. But the Helper, the Holy Spirit, whom the Father will send in my name, he will teach you all things and bring to your remembrance all that I have said to you. (John 14:25-26)

> When the Spirit of truth comes, he will guide you into all the truth, for he will not speak on his own authority, but whatever he hears he will speak, and he will declare to you the things that are to come. He will glorify me, for he will take what is mine and declare it to you. (John 16:13-14)

[50] "In him you also, when you heard the word of truth, the gospel of your salvation, and believed in him, were sealed with the promised Holy Spirit, who is the guarantee of our inheritance until we acquire possession of it, to the praise of his glory." (Ephesians 1:13-14)

[51] "For all who are led by the Spirit of God are sons of God. For you did not receive the spirit of slavery to fall back into fear, but you have received the Spirit of adoption as sons, by whom we cry, 'Abba! Father!' The Spirit himself bears witness with our spirit that we are children of God." (Romans 8:14-16)

[52] See, for example:

> And the disciples were filled with joy and with the Holy Spirit. (Acts 13:52)

> And you became imitators of us and of the Lord, for you received the word in much affliction, with joy inspired by the Holy Spirit. (1 Thessalonians 1:6)

> But the fruit of the Spirit is love, joy, peace, patience, kindness, goodness, faithfulness, gentleness, self-control; against such there is no law. (Galatians 5:22-23)

> For the kingdom of God is not food and drink but righteousness and peace and joy in the Holy Spirit. (Romans 14:17)

[53] 2 Corinthians 13:14. Also: "Go therefore and make disciples of all nations, baptizing them in the name of the Father and of the Son and of the Holy Spirit." (Matthew 28:19)

For "triadic" references to God in New Testament writings, see:

> There is one body and *one Spirit* – just as you were called to the one hope that belongs to your call – *one Lord,* one faith, one baptism, *one God and Father* of all, who is over all and through all and in all." (Ephesians 4:4-6)

Therefore I want you to understand that no one speaking in the *Spirit of God* ever says "Jesus is accursed!" and no one can say "*Jesus is Lord*" except in the *Holy Spirit.* Now there are varieties of gifts, but the same *Spirit*; and there are varieties of service, but the same *Lord*; and there are varieties of activities, but it is the same *God* who empowers them all in everyone. (1 Corinthians 12:3-6)

. . . according to the foreknowledge of *God the Father*, in the sanctification of *the Spirit*, for obedience to *Jesus Christ* and for sprinkling with his blood: May grace and peace be multiplied to you. (1 Peter 1:2)

Blessed be the *God and Father* of our Lord Jesus Christ, who has blessed us in *Christ* with every spiritual blessing in the heavenly places, even as he chose us in him before the foundation of the world, that we should be holy and blameless before him. In love he predestined us for adoption as sons through *Jesus Christ*, according to the purpose of his will, to the praise of his glorious grace, with which he has blessed us in the Beloved. . . . In him you also, when you heard the word of truth, the gospel of your salvation, and believed in him, were sealed with the promised *Holy Spirit*, who is the guarantee of our inheritance until we acquire possession of it, to the praise of his glory. (Ephesians 1:3-14)

For passages in which all three Persons are mentioned together, see:

And when he came up out of the water, immediately he saw the heavens being torn open and *the Spirit* descending on *him* like a dove. And a voice came from heaven, "*You* are *my* beloved *Son*; with *you I* am well pleased." (Mark1:10-11)

But when the fullness of time had come, *God* sent forth his *Son*, born of woman, born under the law, to redeem those who were under the law, so that we might receive adoption as sons. And because you are sons, God has sent the *Spirit* of his *Son* into our hearts, crying, "Abba! *Father*!" (Galatians 4:4-6)

There is therefore now no condemnation for those who are in *Christ Jesus*. For the law of the *Spirit* of life has set you free in *Christ Jesus* from the law of sin and death. For *God* has done what the law, weakened by the flesh, could not do. By sending *his own Son* in the likeness of sinful flesh and for sin, he condemned sin in the flesh, in order that the righteous requirement of the law might be fulfilled in us, who walk not according to the flesh but according to the *Spirit.* (Romans 8:1-4)

But we ought always to give thanks to God for you, brothers beloved by the Lord, because *God* chose you as the firstfruits to be saved, through sanctification by the *Spirit* and belief in the truth. To this he called you through our gospel, so that you may obtain the glory of our *Lord Jesus Christ.* So then, brothers, stand firm and hold to the traditions that you were taught by us, either by our spoken word or by our letter. Now may our Lord Jesus Christ himself, and God our Father, who loved us and gave us eternal comfort and good hope through grace, comfort your hearts and establish them in every good work and word. (2 Thessalonians 2:13-17)

But when the goodness and loving kindness of *God* our Savior appeared, he saved us, not because of works done by us in righteousness, but according to his own mercy, by the washing of regeneration and renewal of the *Holy Spirit*, whom he poured out on us richly through *Jesus Christ* our Savior. (Titus 3:4-6)

But you, beloved, building yourselves up in your most holy faith and praying in the *Holy Spirit,* keep yourselves in the love of *God,* waiting for the mercy of our *Lord Jesus Christ* that leads to eternal life. (Jude 20-21)

[54] J.N.D. Kelly wrote:

> The doctrine of one God, the Father and creator, formed the background and indisputable premiss of the Church's faith. Inherited from Judaism, it was her bulwark against pagan polytheism, Gnostic emanationism and Marcionite dualism. The problem for theology was to integrate with it, intellectually, the fresh data of the specifically Christian revelation. Reduced to their simplest, these were the convictions that God had made Himself known in the Person of Jesus, the Messiah, raising Him from the dead and offering salvation to men through Him, and that He had poured out His Holy Spirit upon the Church. Even at the New Testament stage ideas about Christ's pre-existence and creative role were beginning to take shape, and a profound, if often obscure, awareness of the activity of the Spirit in the Church was emerging. No steps had been taken so far, however, to work all these complex elements into a coherent whole. The Church had to wait for more than three hundred years for a final synthesis. . . . of one God existing in three co-equal Persons. . . ."

J.N.D. Kelly, *Early Christian Doctrines,* Fifth Edition (London, New York NY: Continuum International Publishing Group, 2000), p. 87.

[55] Augustine, "On Christian Doctrine," p. 524.

Following Augustine, the Catholic theologian, M.J. Scheeben, wrote:

> When God graciously adopts us as His children and truly unites us to Himself in a most intimate manner by the grace of sonship . . . He gives us Himself, His own essence, as the object of our delight. . . . In consequence of this presence of the divine essence in the soul and the real union of the soul with God which is effected by grace . . . we enjoy God . . . as an object that is really and truly in us and is our own. We truly grasp Him with our knowledge and embrace Him with our love . . . . God becomes the object of our possession and enjoyment in His entire essence. Evidently, then, all three persons come to us and give themselves to us, inasmuch as they are one with the essence, and in the essence with each other. Yet the individual persons, too, as distinct from one another and especially so far as one proceeds from another, can give themselves to us for our possession and enjoyment.

Quoted in Edmund J. Fortman, S.J., *The Triune God: A Historical Study of the Doctrine of the Trinity* (Philadelphia: The Westminster Press, 1972), p. 306.

[56] For a contemporary call to ground our lives as Christians in the Triune life of God, see Jeff Imbach, *The River Within: Loving God, Living Passionately* (Colorado Springs: NavPress, 1998).

For a philosophical treatment of the Trinity in human experience, see David Brown, *The Divine Trinity* (LaSalle, Illinois: Open Court Publishing Company, 1985), pp. 207ff.

CHAPTER 2: JOY AND THE GLORY OF GOD

1 "And Stephen said: 'Brothers and fathers, hear me. The God of glory appeared to our father Abraham when he was in Mesopotamia, before he lived in Haran.'" (Acts 7:2)

2 "Lift up your heads, O gates!
And be lifted up, O ancient doors,
that the King of glory may come in." (Psalm 24:7)

3 ". . . that the God of our Lord Jesus Christ, the Father of glory, may give you the Spirit of wisdom and of revelation in the knowledge of him." (Ephesians 1:17)

4 "For when he received honor and glory from God the Father, and the voice was borne to him by the Majestic Glory, 'This is my beloved Son, with whom I am well pleased.'" (2 Peter 1:17)

5 If you read *Path of Life*, you may remember this section on the glory of God from the chapter, "Joy and the Good Life." Rick Howe, *Path of Life: Finding the Joy You've Always Longed For* (Boulder, CO: University Ministries Press, 2017).

The Westminster Shorter Catechism tells us that there are two dimensions of our chief end – glorifying God and enjoying him. We do not have two chief ends, but one with two facets (as John Piper observes in his work, *Desiring God: Meditations of a Christian Hedonist* [Portland, Oregon: Multnomah Press, 1986], p. 13. As C.S. Lewis saw it, "Fully to enjoy is to glorify. In commanding us to glorify Him, God is inviting us to enjoy Him." C.S. Lewis, *Reflections on the Psalms* [New York: Harcourt Brace Jovanovich, 1958], p. 97.)

Glorifying God and enjoying him are united in our life before him, because glory and joy are united in God himself. Karl Barth was right:

> God's glory is the indwelling joy of His divine being which as such shines out from Him, which overflows in its richness, which in its super-abundance is not satisfied with itself but communicates itself.
>
> God's glory is His overflowing self-communicating joy. By its very nature it is that which gives joy.
>
> But we cannot overlook the fact that God is glorious in such a way that He radiates joy.

Karl Barth, *Church Dogmatics*, eds., Geoffrey W. Bromiley, T. F. Torrance (New York: Charles Scribner's Sons, 1957), Vol. II, pp. 647, 653, 655.

6 Bernard Ramm calls it "both a modality of the self-revelation of God, and an attribute of God." Bernard Ramm, *Them He Glorified* (Grand Rapids: Eerdmans, 1963), p. 10. Karl Barth wrote: "[God's glory] is God Himself in the truth and capacity and act in which He makes himself known as God." Barth, *Church Dogmatics*, Vol. II, p. 641.

7 "God is spirit, and those who worship him must worship in spirit and truth." (John 4:24)

8 1 Timothy 1:17, RSV

9 ". . . who alone has immortality, who dwells in unapproachable light, whom no one has ever seen or can see. To him be honor and eternal dominion. Amen." (1 Timothy 6:16)

10 For the metaphor of God robing himself, see:

> The LORD reigns; he is robed in majesty. (Psalm 93:1)
>
> Of old you laid the foundation of the earth,
> and the heavens are the work of your hands.
> They will perish, but you will remain;
> they will all wear out like a garment.
> You will change them like a robe, and they will pass away. (Psalm 102:25-26)
>
> Bless the LORD, O my soul!
> O LORD my God, you are very great!
> You are clothed with splendor and majesty,
> covering yourself with light as with a garment. (Psalm 104:1-2)

Calvin quoted this Psalm and then wrote:

> It is as if he said; Thereafter the Lord began to show himself in the *visible splendor of his apparel*, ever since in the creation of the universe he brought forth those insignia *whereby he shows his glory to us*, whenever and wherever we cast our glaze. (Emphasis added.)

John Calvin, *Institutes of the Christian Religion*, ed., John T. McNeill, trans. Ford Lewis Battles (Philadelphia: Westminster, 1960), Vol. 1, p. 52.

11 God appears to mortals in his glory. See, for example:

> Nations will fear the name of the LORD,
> and all the kings of the earth will fear your glory.
> For the Lord builds up Zion;
> *he appears in his glory*; (Psalm 102:15-16)

12 Deism is the view that a supreme being created the universe, but does not interfere in its workings, choosing, instead, to let it run entirely "on its own" according to the laws of nature imbedded in it from its origin.

13 Pantheism is the view that the world and God are identical. If we could see beyond illusions and deceptive appearances we would see that everything is divine.

14 The word "panentheism" literally means "everything-in-God-ism." It is the view that although there is a dimension to God which transcends the cosmos, the cosmos is part of God and exists in God.

15 The universe is "charged with the grandeur of God." Gerard Manley Hopkins, "God's Grandeur," in *Chief Modern Poets of Britain and America*, ed., Gerald DeWitt Sanders, John Herbert Nelson, M.L. Rosenthal (London: The Macmillan Company, 1970), Vol. I, p. 60.

John Walton sees the creation account in Genesis portraying the cosmos as a temple in which God comes to dwell, and through which he makes his glory known. John H Walton, *The Lost World of Genesis One: Ancient Cosmology and the Origins Debate*, (Downers Grove, IL: InterVarsity Press, 2009).

The world as the theater of God's glory was a significant theme in the thought of John Calvin. See "John Calvin and the World as a Theater of God's Glory" in Belden C. Lane, *Ravished by Beauty: The Surprising Legacy of Reformed Spirituality* (Oxford: Oxford University Press, 2011), pp. 57-85.

16 ". . . because they exchanged the truth about God for a lie and worshiped and served the creature rather than the Creator, who is blessed forever! Amen." (Romans 1:25)

17 Quoted in *The Essential Augustine*, ed., Vernon J. Bourke (Indianapolis: Hackett Publishing Company, second printing, 1978), pp. 131-132.

18 In the Scriptures, glory and beauty are often closely related. See, for example:

> And you shall make holy garments for Aaron your brother, for glory and for beauty. (Exodus 28:2)
>
> Give unto the LORD the glory due unto his name: bring an offering, and come before him: worship the LORD in the beauty of holiness. (1 Chronicles 16:29, KJV)
>
> In that day the LORD of hosts will be a crown of glory,
> and a diadem of beauty, to the remnant of his people. (Isaiah 28:5)

19 St. Augustine, "Sermon 241," *The Works of Saint Augustine,* III/7, p. 71.

20 Theologians created a word for this: *theophany*, or a visible manifestation of God.

21 See:

> Now Moses was keeping the flock of his father-in-law, Jethro, the priest of Midian, and he led his flock to the west side of the wilderness and came to Horeb, the mountain of God. And the angel of the LORD appeared to him in a flame of fire out of the midst of a bush. He looked, and behold, the bush was burning, yet it was not consumed. And Moses said, "I will turn aside to see this great sight, why the bush is not burned." When the LORD saw that he turned aside to see, God called to him out of the bush, "Moses, Moses!" And he said, "Here I am." Then he said, "Do not come near; take your sandals off your feet, for the place on which you are standing is holy ground." And he said, "I am the God of your father, the God of Abraham, the God of Isaac, and the God of Jacob." And Moses hid his face, for he was afraid to look at God. (Exodus 3:1-6)

22 See, for example:

> Then the angel of God who was going before the host of Israel moved and went behind them, and the pillar of cloud moved from before them and stood behind them, coming between the host of Egypt and the host of Israel. And there was the cloud and the darkness. And it lit up the night without one coming near the other all night. (Exodus 14:19-20)

> Then Moses went up on the mountain, and the cloud covered the mountain. The glory of the LORD dwelt on Mount Sinai, and the cloud covered it six days. And on the seventh day he called to Moses out of the midst of the cloud. Now the appearance of the glory of the LORD was like a devouring fire on the top of the mountain in the sight of the people of Israel. (Exodus 24:15-17)

23 See the following:

> On the morning of the third day there were thunders and lightnings and a thick cloud on the mountain and a very loud trumpet blast, so that all the people in the camp trembled. (Exodus 19:16)

> Now when all the people saw the thunder and the flashes of lightning and the sound of the trumpet and the mountain smoking, the people were afraid and trembled, and they stood far off and said to Moses, "You speak to us, and we will listen; but do not let God speak to us, lest we die." (Exodus 20:18-19)

> The LORD thundered from heaven,
> and the Most High uttered his voice.
> And he sent out arrows and scattered them;
> lightning, and routed them. (2 Samuel 22:14-15)

24 "Then the cloud covered the tent of meeting, and the glory of the LORD filled the tabernacle." (Exodus 40:34)

25 Jewish rabbis used the word "Shekinah" to describe the glory of God in his dwelling among humans. See Gerhard Kittel, ed., *Theological Dictionary of the New Testament*, trans. Geoffrey W. Bromiley (Grand Rapids, MI: Wm. B. Eerdmans Publishing Co., 1964), Vol. II, pp. 245-46.

26 In addition to the theme of divine glory in the Scriptures, we should add God's spoken word. He speaks in many ways (Hebrews 1:1). It may be an audible voice or an inner word. He may speak in a dream or a vision. His word may come to us directly, or through someone else he brings into our lives. Just as we hold ourselves in a state of readiness for glory, we should anticipate ways in which God may address us with a word. The posture of our hearts throughout the day ought to be, "Speak, LORD, for your servant is listening." (1 Samuel 3:9)

27 See:

> Blessed be the God and Father of our Lord Jesus Christ, the Father of mercies and God of all comfort. (2 Corinthians 1:3)

The God and Father of the Lord Jesus, he who is blessed forever, knows that I am not lying. (2 Corinthians 11:31)

Blessed be the God and Father of our Lord Jesus Christ, who has blessed us in Christ with every spiritual blessing in the heavenly places. (Ephesians 1:3)

28 In the Hymn, *This is My Father's World*, we sing, "In the rustling grass I hear him pass." Not all grass that moves in the wind bears his presence to us, but it can and might!

29 Psalm 40:16

30 See, for example:

You will seek me and find me, when you seek me with all your heart. (Jeremiah 29:13)

I love those who love me,
and those who seek me diligently find me. (Proverbs 8:17)

Without faith it is impossible to please him, for whoever would draw near to God must believe that he exists and that he rewards those who seek him. (Hebrews 11:6)

31 Exodus 33:18-19, NRSV. 2 Peter 1:3 links the glory of God and the goodness of God: "His divine power has given us everything we need for a godly life through our knowledge of him who called us by his own glory and goodness." (NIV)

32 Ramm, *Them He Glorified*, pp. 20-21.

33 See:

One thing have I asked of the LORD,
  that will I seek after;
that I may dwell in the house of the LORD
  all the days of my life,
to behold the beauty of the LORD,
  and to inquire in his temple. (Psalm 27:4, RSV)

34 Jürgen Moltmann, *Theology and Joy*, trans. Reinhard Ulrich (London: SCM Press, LTD, 1973), p. 62. Speaking of joy and the beauty of God, Karl Barth wrote: "He has it as a fact and a power in such a way that He acts as the One who gives pleasure, creates desire and rewards with enjoyment, because He is the One who is pleasant, desirable, full of enjoyment, because first and last He alone is that which is pleasant, desirable and full of enjoyment." Barth, *Church Dogmatics*, Vol. II, Part 1, p. 651.

35 A.W. Tozer, *Whatever Happened to Worship?* ed., Gerald B. Smith (Camp Hill, Pennsylvania: Christian Publications, 1985), p. 28.

You may wonder why I include theologians who, apart from their interest in joy, have little in common. Moltmann and Tozer? Joy is a gift that is given without respect to theological conventions. It has the potential to unite people despite their theological differences. Joy is an ecumenical force. Those who experience joy do their best to describe it with the theological grammar and vocabulary at hand.

36 2 Corinthians 3:18

37 Jonathan Edwards, "Dissertation Concerning The End for Which God Created the World," in *The Works of Jonathan Edwards* (Philadelphia: The Banner of Truth Trust, 1984), Vol. I, p. 101.

38 "And we all, with unveiled face, beholding the glory of the Lord, are being transformed into the same image from one degree of glory to another. For this comes from the Lord who is the Spirit." (2 Corinthians 3:18)

39 "Will not the ministry of the Spirit have even more glory?" (2 Corinthians 3:8)

40 See:

> But Saul, still breathing threats and murder against the disciples of the Lord, went to the high priest and asked him for letters to the synagogues at Damascus, so that if he found any belonging to the Way, men or women, he might bring them bound to Jerusalem. Now as he went on his way, he approached Damascus, and suddenly a light from heaven shone around him. And falling to the ground he heard a voice saying to him, 'Saul, Saul, why are you persecuting me?' And he said, 'Who are you, Lord?' And he said, 'I am Jesus, whom you are persecuting. But rise and enter the city, and you will be told what you are to do.' The men who were traveling with him stood speechless, hearing the voice but seeing no one. Saul rose from the ground, and although his eyes were opened, he saw nothing. So they led him by the hand and brought him into Damascus. And for three days he was without sight, and neither ate nor drank. (Acts 9:1-9)

41 " For it is the God who said, 'Let light shine out of darkness,' who has shone in our hearts to give the light of the knowledge of the glory of God in the face of Christ." (2 Corinthians 4:6, RSV)

42 "Holy, holy, holy is the LORD of hosts; the whole earth is full of his glory!" (Isaiah 6:3)

43 "Though you have not seen him, you love him. Though you do not now see him, you believe in him and rejoice with joy that is inexpressible and filled with glory." (1 Peter 1:8)

44 "The heavens declare the glory of God,
and the sky above proclaims his handiwork." (Psalm 19:1)

45 "And we all, with unveiled face, beholding the glory of the Lord, are being transformed into the same image from one degree of glory to another. For this comes from the Lord who is the Spirit." (2 Corinthians 3:18)

46 1 Peter 1:8

47 The Incarnation itself is the greatest Divine Visitation. The reality of Incarnation ("This is my Son, whom I love; with him I am well pleased.") was disclosed dramatically in this episodic Visitation.

48 But not after it. As great as the glory of the Transfiguration must have been, the glory of the risen and ascended Christ is far greater! The apostle Paul was blinded by it (Acts 9:1-9), and John fell as a dead man after his encounter with it (Revelation 1:9-20).

49 In a story placed just before the Transfiguration, Jesus had this very important conversation with his disciples:

> Now it happened that as he was praying alone, the disciples were with him. And he asked them, "Who do the crowds say that I am?" And they answered, "John the Baptist. But others say, Elijah, and others that one of the prophets of old has risen." Then he said to them, "But who do you say that I am?" And Peter answered, "The Christ of God." (Luke 9:18-20)

50 "And the Word became flesh and dwelt among us, and we have seen his glory, glory as of the only Son from the Father, full of grace and truth." (John 1:14)

Chapter 3: Enjoying God's World

1 "... when the morning stars sang together
and all the sons of God shouted for joy?" (Job 38:7)

This inspired C.S. Lewis in his story of the creation of Narnia. In *The Magician's Nephew*, Lewis wrote:

> In the darkness something was happening at last. A voice had begun to sing. It was very far away and Digory found it hard to decide from what direction it was coming. Sometimes it seemed to come from all directions at once. Sometimes he almost thought it was coming out of the earth beneath them. Its lower notes were deep enough to be the voice of the earth herself. There were no words. There was hardly even a tune. But it was, beyond comparison, the most beautiful noise he had ever heard. It was so beautiful he could hardly bear it. . . .
> Then two wonders happened at the same moment. One was that the voice [of Aslan] was suddenly joined by other voices; more voices than you could possibly count. They were in harmony with it, but far higher up the scale: cold, tingling, silver voices. The second wonder was that the blackness overhead, all at once, was blazing with stars. They didn't come out gently one by one, as they do on a summer evening. One moment there had been nothing but darkness; next moment a thousand, thousand points of light leaped out – single stars, constellations, and planets, brighter and bigger than any in our world. There were no clouds. The new stars and the new voices began at exactly the same time. If you had seen and heard it, as Digory did, you would have felt quite certain that it was the stars themselves which were singing, and that it was the First Voice, the deep one, which had made them appear and made them sing.

C.S. Lewis, *The Magician's Nephew* (New York: NY, HarperTrophy, 1983), pp. 116-117.

2 In Anselmian terms, God is that than which no greater can be conceived. He is supreme in every conceivable way.

3 "He was free to create or not to create. He did it out of his own good pleasure, for the divine fun of it." Louis Smedes, "Theology and the Playful Life," in *God and the Good: Essays in Honor of Henry Stob*, eds., Clifton Orlebeke and Lewis Smedes (Grand Rapids: William B. Eerdmans Publishing Co. 1975), p. 56.

We see the Creator's joy in his creative work first in his benedictions over it: "And God saw that it was *good.*" (Genesis 1:10, 12, 18, 21, 25, 31)

4 See, for example, Psalm 103:1-5; 107:9; James 1:17.

5 See "The Highest and Best of All Pleasures" in Rick Howe, *Path of Life: Finding the Joy You've Always Longed For* (Boulder, CO: University Ministries Press, 2017). My primary thesis there is that joy is the highest and best of life's pleasures, and the one Pleasure that embraces and enhances all other pleasures given by God.

6 Martin Luther, *The Table Talk of Martin Luther,* ed., Thomas S. Kepler (Grand Rapids: Baker Book House, 1952, reprint., 1979), pp. 40-41.

7 Peter Kreeft, *Heaven: The Heart's Deepest Longing* (San Francisco: Ignatius Press, 1989), p. 111.

8 See also:

> Yet he is not far from each one of us, for 'in him we live and move and have our being.' (Acts 17:27-28, RSV)
>
> Ever since the creation of the world his invisible nature, namely, his eternal power and deity, has been clearly perceived in the things that have been made. (Romans 1:20, RSV)

9 See:

> Where shall I go from your Spirit?
>   Or where shall I flee from your presence?
> If I ascend to heaven, you are there!
>   If I make my bed in Sheol, you are there!
> If I take the wings of the morning
>   and dwell in the uttermost parts of the sea,
> even there your hand shall lead me,
>   and your right hand shall hold me.
> If I say, 'Surely the darkness shall cover me,
>   and the light about me be night,'
> even the darkness is not dark to you;
>   the night is bright as the day,
>   for darkness is as light with you. (Psalm 139:7-12)

10 For a recent treatment of the immanence of God as the presence and work of the Spirit, see Clark Pinnock, *Flame of Love: A Theology of the Holy Spirit* (Downers Grove, Illinois: InterVarsity Press, 1996), especially chapter 2.

11 Calvin wrote:

> Men cannot open their eyes without being compelled to see him. Indeed, his essence is incomprehensible; hence, his divineness far escapes all human perception. But upon his individual works he has engraved unmistakable marks of his glory. . . . ever since in the creation of the universe he brought forth those insignia whereby he shows his glory to us, whenever and wherever we cast our gaze.

John Calvin, *Institutes of the Christian Religion*, ed., John T. McNeill, trans. Fort Lewis Battles (Philadelphia: The Westminster Press, 1960), Vol. I, p. 52.

12 C.S. Lewis, *Letters to Malcolm: Chiefly on Prayer* (New York: Harcourt Brace Jovanovich, Inc., 1963), pp. 89-90.

13 C.S. Lewis wrote: "God whispers to us in our pleasures, speaks in our conscience, but shouts in our pains." C.S. Lewis, *The Problem of Pain*, New York: Collier Books, Macmillan Publishing Company, 1962), p. 93.

14 Luther, *Table Talk*, p. 67. Emphasis added.

15 John Calvin, *Institutes of the Christian Religion*, trans. Henry Beveridge (Grand Rapids: William B. Eerdmans Publishing Co., 1979), Vol. I, p. 157. Emphasis added.

16 Nicholas Wolterstorff, *Art in Action: Toward a Christian Aesthetic* (Grand Rapids: William B. Eerdmans Publishing Co., 1980), p. 72.

17 Arthur F. Holmes, *Contours of a World View* (Grand Rapids: William B. Eerdmans Publishing Co., 1983), p. 67.

18 C.S. Lewis, *Mere Christianity* (New York: Macmillan Publishing Co., Inc., 1960 ed.) p. 65.

19 C.S. Lewis, "The Weight of Glory" in *The Weight of Glory and Other Addresses* (Grand Rapids: William B. Eerdmans Publishing Co., 1949, reprint. 1974), p. 14.

20 "Man is neither angel nor brute." *Pascal's Pensèes*, trans. W.F. Trotter, (New York: E.P. Dutton & Co., Inc., 1958), p. 99.

21 "I fancy the 'beauties of nature' are a secret God has shared with us alone. That may be one of the reasons why we were made. . . ." C.S. Lewis, *Letters to Malcolm: Chiefly on Prayer* (New York: Harcourt Brace Jovanovich, Inc., 1963), p. 18.

Elsewhere Lewis wrote:

> The angels have not senses; their experience is purely intellectual and spiritual. That is why we know something about God which they don't. There are particular aspects of His love and joy which can be communicated to a created being only by sensuous experience. Something of God which the seraphim can never quite understand flows into us from the blue sky, the taste of honey, the delicious embrace of water whether cold or hot, or even from sleep itself.

C.S. Lewis, "Scraps" in *God in the Dock: Essays on Theology and Ethics* (Grand Rapids: William B. Eerdmans Publishing Co., 1975), p. 216.

22 While I acknowledge that contemporary genetic evidence and other postulates of evolutionary theory represent a challenge that should engage Christians in serious thinking and dialogue, I did not come to my belief (nor will I abandon my belief) in a historical Adam and Eve, an original Edenic environment in which they lived, and a state of innocence from which they fell, on the basis of scientific inquiry.

The Scriptures are the "norming norm" for my faith. I make no apologies for this. Indeed, it is a great joy to me! Having said this, the ancient texts of Scripture must be read first – as much as possible – with their original audience in mind. We should resist the temptation of importing our interests and concerns into the way we understand them, and forcing them to take up arms in our conflicts.

I recognize that the Hebrew word *adam* was used for humanity as a whole as well as for an individual in the Genesis story (Adam = Mankind). I can also see how Israel, in its exile from the promised land, would have seen itself in Adam and his expulsion from the

Garden (Adam = Israel). Neither of these observations, however, negates the possibility that Adam was *also* viewed as a historical figure. (Compare Jacob = Israel.) Neither seems to factor into the canonical context of Jesus' teaching on marriage and divorce in Matthew 19, and Paul's exposition of redemptive history in Romans 5 – both of which posit a historical Adam.

While Jesus does not refer to an original pair by name, his affirmation of the Creator's original intention for marriage clearly has the Edenic couple in mind. ("He who created them from the beginning made them male and female, and said, 'Therefore a man shall leave his father and his mother and hold fast to his wife, and the two shall become one flesh.'" On the matter of divorce, he affirms an original state of innocence from which humanity has lapsed ("From the beginning it was not so.")

In Romans 5, Israel as a nation is not in view. The "one man" (Adam) is distinguished from all who followed from him ("all men"). In this passage we do observe the Jewish penchant for seeing deeper meanings in their stories. Adam is not an archetype for humanity or for Israel, however, but a "type" of Christ. This is the frame of reference in which we should pursue our interpretation. The parallels are between two men (Adam and Christ), sin entering the world through one and grace through the other, an act of disobedience and an act of righteousness, judgment and justification, death and eternal life. Any other frame of reference is alien to the context. In a grand metanarrative, Paul lays out the themes of Creation, Fall, and Redemption: one man in the beginning from whom humanity sprang and through whose "act of disobedience" sin entered the world, a historical period ("from Adam to Moses"), and God's saving action through the one man, Jesus Christ ("the one who was to come").

I affirm that there is great value in the scientific enterprise, and believe that if we love God with our minds (in fulfillment of the greatest commandment) we will boldly declare that all truth is his – wherever it is found – and we will pursue it to the best of our abilities under God. I also affirm the priority and supremacy of the Scriptures for our faith, and what seems to me to be the clear teaching of Jesus and Paul. This leads me to a confident belief that whatever we may say about the age of the universe and the development of life on our planet, there was an original couple who bore the image of God without flaw, were placed in an Edenic setting of innocence, fell from that state through a primal act of disobedience, and brought sin into the world as well as all future generations of humans who fallibly bear the image of God.

For a contemporary discussion, see Matthew Barrett and Ardel B. Caneday, eds. *Four Views on the Historical Adam* (Grand Rapids: Zondervan, 2013).

23 See, for example:

> I said in my heart, "Come now, I will test you with pleasure; enjoy yourself." But behold, this also was vanity. I said of laughter, "It is mad," and of pleasure, "What use is it?" I searched with my heart how to cheer my body with wine – my heart still guiding me with wisdom – and how to lay hold on folly, till I might see what was good for the children of man to do under heaven during the few days of their life. I made great works. I built houses and planted vineyards for myself. I made myself gardens and parks, and planted in them all kinds of fruit trees. I made myself pools from which to water the forest of growing trees. I bought male and female slaves, and had slaves who were

born in my house. I had also great possessions of herds and flocks, more than any who had been before me in Jerusalem. I also gathered for myself silver and gold and the treasure of kings and provinces. I got singers, both men and women, and many concubines, the delight of the sons of man. So I became great and surpassed all who were before me in Jerusalem. Also my wisdom remained with me. And whatever my eyes desired I did not keep from them. I kept my heart from no pleasure, for my heart found pleasure in all my toil, and this was my reward for all my toil. Then I considered all that my hands had done and the toil I had expended in doing it, and behold, all was vanity and a striving after wind, and there was nothing to be gained under the sun." (Ecclesiastes 2:1-11)

And as for what fell among the thorns, they are those who hear, but as they go on their way they are choked by the cares and riches and pleasures of life, and their fruit does not mature. (Luke 8:14)

But she who is self-indulgent is dead even while she lives. (1 Timothy 5:6)

[They are] treacherous, reckless, swollen with conceit, lovers of pleasure rather than lovers of God. (2 Timothy 3:4)

For we ourselves were once foolish, disobedient, led astray, slaves to various passions and pleasures, passing our days in malice and envy, hated by others and hating one another. (Titus 3:3)

24 Augustine, "Confessions" in *The Basic Writings of Saint Augustine,* ed., Whitney J. Oates (Grand Rapids: Baker Book House, 1948, reprinted 1980), p. 179. I have changed the King James pronouns and verbal endings to a contemporary idiom.

25 C.S. Lewis, *The Problem of Pain* , pp. 79-80.

26 "Now the Spirit expressly says that in later times some will depart from the faith by giving heed to deceitful spirits and doctrines of demons, through the pretensions of liars whose consciences are seared." (1 Timothy 4:1-2)

27 1 Timothy 4:4-5, NASB

28 C.S. Lewis, *Letters to Malcolm*, p. 89

29 Although it is incomplete because its only factors are creation and fall, Emil Brunner is worth quoting: "Since Creation comes first, and sin comes second, the primary duty of man is to adopt a positive attitude towards life - an attitude of affirmation, acceptance, and adjustment to its claims; the negative attitude of denial takes the second place." Emil Brunner, *The Divine Imperative,* trans. Olive Wyon, (The Westminster Press: Philadelphia, 1947), p. 126.

30 See, for example, the following:

For behold, I create new heavens
  and a new earth,
and the former things shall not be remembered
  or come into mind.

But be glad and rejoice forever
in that which I create;
for behold, I create Jerusalem to be a joy,
and her people to be a gladness.
I will rejoice in Jerusalem
and be glad in my people;
no more shall be heard in it the sound of weeping
and the cry of distress. (Isaiah 65:17-19)

. . . waiting for and hastening the coming of the day of God, because of which the heavens will be set on fire and dissolved, and the heavenly bodies will melt as they burn! But according to his promise we are waiting for new heavens and a new earth in which righteousness dwells. (2 Peter 3:12-13)

Then I saw a new heaven and a new earth, for the first heaven and the first earth had passed away, and the sea was no more. (Revelation 21:1)

31 Diogenes Allen captured the essence of this tension:

> To forsake the world is not to reject the world. To forsake the world is to realize that there is nothing you know of, have experienced, or can imagine, which would satisfy you.
>
> This attitude is perfectly compatible with a recognition of the glories of the world, its radiant beauty, its delights, its satisfactions, its wonders, and all the rest.
>
> Forsaking the world is an attitude. That is, it can exist alongside laughter, hearty fun, delight in a child, a full and active life. It does not drive everything else out, as does a mood. It does not rob things of value.

Diogenes Allen, *Finding Our Father* (Atlanta: John Knox Press, 1974), pp. 78-79.

Karl Barth captures something of this dialectic of "yes" and "no" in our joy:

> What is here regarded as joy, and is this, has obviously passed through a catalysator. It has been destroyed on the one hand, and reconstituted on the other. But it has been reconstituted, and validated, and even raised to the level of a command. Christ is risen; He is truly risen. Joy is now joy before the Lord and in Him. It is joy in His salvation, His grace, His law, His whole action. But it is now genuine, earthly, human joy: the joy of harvest, wedding, festival and victory; the joy not only of the inner but of the outer man; the joy in which one may and must drink wine as well as eat bread, sing and play as well as speak, dance as well as pray.

Karl Barth, *Church Dogmatics*, trans., Mr. A.T. Mackay, et. al. (Edinburgh: T. & T. Clark, 1961) Volume III, 4, pp. 375-376.

32 This is another way of saying, as Aquinas did, that there is a rational, as well as a sensory dimension, to human pleasure:

> Pleasure arises from union with a suitable object perceived or known.

Three things are requisite for pleasure; two, i.e., the one that is pleased and the pleasurable object conjoined to him; and a third, which is knowledge of this conjunction.

Thomas Aquinas, *Summa Theologica* I, II, Q. 31, A. 5 and Q. 32. A. 1.

33 St. Augustine, "City of God" in *Basic Writings of Saint Augustine*, ed. Whitney J. Oates (New York: Random House Publishers, 1948) Vol. II, p. 108. Emphasis added.

34 Aquinas, *Summa Theologica*, I, I, Q. 5, A.4. Emphasis added.

35 David Elton Trueblood, *Philosophy of Religion* (Grand Rapids: Baker Book House, 1957), p. 120. Emphasis added.

36 C.S. Lewis, *Letters to Malcolm*, pp. 89-90.

37 See:

For the wrath of God is revealed from heaven against all ungodliness and unrighteousness of men, who by their unrighteousness suppress the truth. For what can be known about God is plain to them, because God has shown it to them. For his invisible attributes, namely, his eternal power and divine nature, have been clearly perceived, ever since the creation of the world, in the things that have been made. So they are without excuse. For although they knew God, they did not honor him as God or give thanks to him, but they became futile in their thinking, and their foolish hearts were darkened. Claiming to be wise, they became fools, and exchanged the glory of the immortal God for images resembling mortal man and birds and animals and creeping things. Therefore God gave them up in the lusts of their hearts to impurity, to the dishonoring of their bodies among themselves, because they exchanged the truth about God for a lie and worshiped and served the creature rather than the Creator, who is blessed forever! Amen. For this reason God gave them up to dishonorable passions. For their women exchanged natural relations for those that are contrary to nature; and the men likewise gave up natural relations with women and were consumed with passion for one another, men committing shameless acts with men and receiving in themselves the due penalty for their error. And since they did not see fit to acknowledge God, God gave them up to a debased mind to do what ought not to be done." (Romans 1:18-28)

38 Martin Luther, "Lectures on Genesis," in *Luther's Works*, ed., Jaroslav Pelikan (Saint Louis: Concordia Publishing House, 1960), Vol. II, p. 348.

39 "Do not be conformed to this world, but be transformed by the renewal of your mind, that by testing you may discern what is the will of God, what is good and acceptable and perfect." (Romans 12:2)

40 1 Timothy 4:3-5. See also:

Now the Spirit expressly says that in later times some will depart from the faith by devoting themselves to deceitful spirits and teachings of demons, through the insincerity of liars whose consciences are seared, who forbid marriage and require abstinence from foods that God created to *be received with thanksgiving by those who*

> *believe and know the truth.* For everything created by God is good, and nothing is to be rejected if it is received with thanksgiving, for it is made holy by the word of God and prayer. (1 Timothy 4:1-5)

41 We live out our days enveloped by the *sacramentum mundi* (the sacrament of the world, or the world as sacrament.)

42 John Walton sees the creation account in Genesis portraying the cosmos as a temple in which God comes to dwell, and through which he makes his glory known. John H Walton, *The Lost World of Genesis One: Ancient Cosmology and the Origins Debate*, (Downers Grove, IL: InterVarsity Press, 2009).

The world as the theater of God's glory was a significant theme in the thought of John Calvin. See "John Calvin and the World as a Theater of God's Glory" in Belden C. Lane, *Ravished by Beauty: The Surprising Legacy of Reformed Spirituality* (Oxford: Oxford University Press, 2011), pp. 57-85.

For explorations of stewarding the earth in a Christian vision of life, see: Steven Bouma-Prediger, *For the Beauty of the Earth: A Christian Vision for Creation Care* (Grand Rapids, MI: Baker Academic, 2001); Wesley Granberg-Michaelson, ed., *Tending the Garden: Essays on the Gospel and the Earth* (Grand Rapids, MI: Eerdmans, 1987); James A. Nash, *Loving Nature: Ecological Integrity and Christian Responsibility* (Nashville: Abingdon, 1993); Francis A. Schaeffer, *Pollution and the Death of Man: The Christian View of Ecology* (Wheaton, IL: Tyndale House, 1970); Loren Wilkinson, ed., *Earthkeeping in the '90s: Stewardship of Creation* (Grand Rapids, MI: Eerdmans, 1990) .

43 With future generations in mind, our responsible use of the world's resources should include renewable energy as much as possible. It is tragic when, through our governments, we rack up debts that will crush future generations, and tragic when we deplete the resources of the earth, or carelessly overuse fossil fuels, leaving future generations in peril. We should oppose both economic policies and energy policies that endanger those who come after us.

44 See:

> "Teacher, which is the great commandment in the Law?" And he said to him, "You shall love the Lord your God with all your heart and with all your soul and with all your mind. This is the great and first commandment. And a second is like it: You shall love your neighbor as yourself. On these two commandments depend all the Law and the Prophets." (Matthew 22:36-40)

Chapter 4: The Joy of Salvation

1 A literal rendering of the name of the Garden in *The Septuagint*, the ancient Greek Translation of the Hebrew Scriptures.

2 Karl Barth wrote of God and creation, "Although he did not create it divine, He did not create it ungodly, or anti-godly, but in harmony and peace with Himself, and therefore, according to His plan, as the theatre and instrument of His acts, an object of His joy and for participation in this joy." Karl Barth, *Church Dogmatics*, eds., G.W. Bromiley, T.F. Torrance (London, New York: T & T Clark International, 2004), Vol. 3.1, p. 102.

3 C.S. Lewis, *Mere Christianity* (New York: Macmillan Publishing Co., Inc., 1960 ed.), p. 52. Emphasis added.

Peter Van Inwagen writes:

> Human beings have not been made merely to mouth words of praise or to be passively awash in a pleasant sensation of the presence of God. They have been made to be intimately aware of God and capable of freely acting on this awareness; having seen God, they may either glorify and enjoy what they have seen -- the glorification and the enjoyment are separate only by the intellect in an act of severe abstraction -- or they may reject what they have seen and attempt to order their own lives and to create their own objects of enjoyment. The choice is theirs and it is a free choice: to choose either way is genuinely open to each human being.
>
> God wishes to be the object of human glorification and enjoyment not out of vanity, but out of love: He is glorious and enjoyable to a degree infinitely greater than that of any other object. He has given us free will in this matter because it is only when a person, having contemplated the properties of something, freely assents to the proposition that that thing is worthy of glory, and then proceeds freely to offer glory to it, that a thing is truly glorified. And it is only when a person, having enjoyed a thing, freely chooses to continue in the enjoyment of that thing that true enjoyment occurs.

Peter Van Inwagen, "Non Est Hick" in *The Rationality of Belief & the Plurality of Faith*, Thomas D. Senor, ed., (Ithica and London: Cornell University Press, 1995), pp. 220-221.

4 It may be true, as Shakespeare put it, that "to err is human," but this is only true of us in our fallenness. We must never understand this to be the case with humanity-as-created-by-God.

5 Psalm 16:4, RSV

6 See:

> Be appalled, O heavens, at this,
> be shocked, be utterly desolate,
> says the LORD,
> for my people have committed two evils;

they have forsaken me,
the fountain of living waters,
and hewed out cisterns for themselves,
broken cisterns,
that can hold no water. (Jeremiah 2:10-13)

7 "For the love of money is a root of all kinds of evils. It is through this craving that some have wandered away from the faith and pierced themselves with many pangs." (1 Timothy 6:10)

8 See

> I said in my heart, "Come now, I will test you with pleasure; enjoy yourself." But behold, this also was vanity. I said of laughter, "It is mad," and of pleasure, "What use is it?" I searched with my heart how to cheer my body with wine—my heart still guiding me with wisdom—and how to lay hold on folly, till I might see what was good for the children of man to do under heaven during the few days of their life. I made great works. I built houses and planted vineyards for myself. I made myself gardens and parks, and planted in them all kinds of fruit trees. I made myself pools from which to water the forest of growing trees. I bought male and female slaves, and had slaves who were born in my house. I had also great possessions of herds and flocks, more than any who had been before me in Jerusalem. I also gathered for myself silver and gold and the treasure of kings and provinces. I got singers, both men and women, and many concubines, the delight of the sons of man. So I became great and surpassed all who were before me in Jerusalem. Also my wisdom remained with me. And whatever my eyes desired I did not keep from them. I kept my heart from no pleasure, for my heart found pleasure in all my toil, and this was my reward for all my toil. (Ecclesiastes 2:1-10)

9 Peter Kreeft, *Heaven: The Heart's Deepest Longing* (San Francisco: Ignatius Press, Expanded edition, 1980), p. 21.

10 "But the serpent said to the woman, 'You will not surely die. For God knows that when you eat of it your eyes will be opened, and you will be like God, knowing good and evil.'" (Genesis 3:5)

11 Ephesians 2:3

12 The wrath of God is more than this. It includes his hatred of sin, his anger towards sin, and his judgment of sin. In Romans 1, however, God, in his wrath, withdraws and leaves us with the consequences of his absence and the presence of our sin. That is what hell will be with finality. The result of wrath for us is the loss of joy, and that is the worst of all possible punishments!

13 Kreeft, *Heaven*, p. 135.

14 ". . . while the sons of the kingdom will be thrown into the outer darkness. In that place there will be weeping and gnashing of teeth." (Matthew 8:12)

15 "You make known to me the path of life;
in your presence there is fullness of joy;

at your right hand are pleasures forevermore." (Psalm 16:11)

16 "They will suffer the punishment of eternal destruction, away from the presence of the Lord and from the glory of his might." (2 Thessalonians 1:9)

17 The sorrow of hell is unending because the sin of choosing another god is ongoing. C.S. Lewis wrote: "I willingly believe that the damned are, in one sense, successful, rebels to the end; that the doors of hell are locked on the inside." C.S. Lewis, *The Problem of Pain* (New York: Macmillan, 1962), p. 127.

18 C.S. Lewis wrote:

> There are only two kinds of people in the end: those who say to God, "Thy will be done," and those to whom God says, in the end, "Thy will be done." All that are in Hell, choose it. Without that self-choice there could be no Hell. No soul that seriously and constantly desires joy will ever miss it. Those who seek find. To those who knock it is opened.

C.S. Lewis, *The Great Divorce* (San Francisco: HarperCollins, 2001), p. 75.

19 "Restore to me the joy of your salvation." (Psalm 51:12)

20 ". . . and hope does not put us to shame, because God's love has been poured into our hearts through the Holy Spirit who has been given to us." (Romans 5:5)

21 Robert Kolb and Timothy J. Wenger eds. *The Book of Concord: The Confessions of the Evangelical Lutheran Church*, trans. Charles Arand, et al (Minneapolis: Fortress Press, 2000), p. 23.

22 Jürgen Moltmann asks this question, and finds its answer in the freedom, good will and love of God. See Jürgen Moltmann, *Theology and Joy,* trans. Reinhard Ulrich (London: SCM Press, 1973), pp. 47ff.

23 Micah 7:18

24 Luke 12:32. "The Kingdom of God stands as a comprehensive term for all that the messianic salvation included." George Eldon Ladd, *A Theology of the New Testament* (Grand Rapids: William B. Eerdmans Publishing Co., 1974), p. 72.

25 Luke 15:7, 23-25, RSV

26 Hebrews 12:2, RSV

27 Hebrews 2:10, 14-15, NRSV

28 ". . . for it is God who works in you, both to will and to work for his good pleasure." (Philippians 2:13)

29 See:

> Now there was a man of the Pharisees named Nicodemus, a ruler of the Jews. This man came to Jesus by night and said to him, "Rabbi, we know that you are a teacher come from God, for no one can do these signs that you do unless God is with him." Jesus answered him, "Truly, truly, I say to you, unless one is born again he cannot see the kingdom of God." Nicodemus said to him, "How can a man be born when he is old? Can he enter a second time into his mother's womb and be born?" Jesus answered, "Truly, truly, I say to you, unless one is born of water and the Spirit, he cannot enter the kingdom of God. That which is born of the flesh is flesh, and that which is born of the Spirit is spirit. Do not marvel that I said to you, 'You must be born again.' The wind blows where it wishes, and you hear its sound, but you do not know where it comes from or where it goes. So it is with everyone who is born of the Spirit." (John 3:1-8)

30 2 Corinthians 5:17

31 A.W. Tozer, *Whatever Happened to Worship?* ed., Gerald B. Smith (Camp Hill, Pennsylvania: Christian Publications, 1985), p. 25.

The Heidelberg Catechism captures this sense of joy as well. It asks, "What is the birth of the new self?" And then answers, "Complete joy in God through Christ and a strong desire to live according to the will of God in all good works." "The Heidelberg Confession," in *The Book of Confessions* (United States: The General Assembly of the United Presbyterian Church in the United States of America, 1967). Q. 90.

32 C.S. Lewis wrote, "For this tangled absurdity of a Need . . . which never fully acknowledges its own neediness, Grace substitutes a full, childlike and delighted acceptance of our Need, a joy in total dependence. We become 'jolly beggars.'" C.S. Lewis, *The Four Loves* (New York: Harcourt, Brace, Jovanovich, 1960), p. 180.

33 C.S. Lewis, *Mere Christianity*, p. 52.

34 Luke 1:46-47

35 C.S. Lewis' way of describing the Trinity. See Chapter 24, "The Three-Personal God" in his *Mere Christianity*.

36 Josef Pieper wrote, "All love has joy as its natural fruit." Josef Pieper, *About Love* (Chicago: Franciscan Herald Press, 1974), p. 71. David Gill speaks of joy as "love's delight." See David W. Gill, *Becoming Good: Building Moral Character* (Downers Grove, Illinois: InterVarsity Press, 2000), p. 54.

37 Jonathan Edwards, "On Religious Affections," *The Works of Jonathan Edwards,* Perry Miller, Gen. ed., (New Haven: Yale University Press, 1959), Vol. 2, p. 114.

38 C.S. Lewis, *God in the Dock: Essays on Theology and Ethics,* ed., Walter Hooper (Grand Rapids: Eerdmans Publishing Co., 1970, reprint., 1976), p. 112.

39 C.S. Lewis, *The Weight of Glory and other Addresses* (Grand Rapids: Eerdmans Publishing Co., 1949, reprint. 1974), p. 14.

40 1 Peter 1:8. NASB

41 "Through him we have also obtained access by faith into this grace in which we stand, and we rejoice in hope of the glory of God. Not only that, but we rejoice in our sufferings, knowing that suffering produces endurance." (Romans 5:2-3)

42 Hebrews 6:5

43 Jonathan Edwards, "On Religious Affections," p. 113.

44 See:

> And not only the creation, but we ourselves, who have the firstfruits of the Spirit, groan inwardly as we wait eagerly for adoption as sons, the redemption of our bodies. (Romans 8:23)
>
> It is sown a natural body; it is raised a spiritual body. If there is a natural body, there is also a spiritual body. (1 Corinthians 15:44)

45 Ephesians 1:14. See also: "He has put his seal upon us and given us his Spirit in our hearts as a guarantee." (2 Corinthians 1:22, RSV)

46 "And not only the creation, but we ourselves, who have the firstfruits of the Spirit, groan inwardly as we wait eagerly for adoption as sons, the redemption of our bodies." (Romans 8:23)

47 The notion of justification should be understood in this framework. It is the verdict of the eschatological judgment rendered in advance because of what Christ has already done. We are declared righteous now in anticipation of the judicial pronouncement that will be made at the end of days.

48 Hebrews 11:16

49 Hebrews 12:22

50 Hebrews 6:5

51 Galatians 1:4

52 George Eldon Ladd, *A Theology of the New Testament* (Grand Rapids, MI: William B. Eerdmans Publishing Co., 1974) p. 69.

53 2 Corinthians 6:9-10

54 See:

> Yet among the mature we do impart wisdom, although it is not a wisdom of this age or of the rulers of this age, who are doomed to pass away. But we impart a secret and hidden wisdom of God, which God decreed before the ages for our glory. None of the

> rulers of this age understood this, for if they had, they would not have crucified the Lord of glory. (1 Corinthians 2:6-8)

55 "But in fact Christ has been raised from the dead, the firstfruits of those who have fallen asleep." (1 Corinthians 15:20)

Speaking of the resurrection of Christ, Moltmann says, "Here indeed begins the laughing of the redeemed, the dancing of the liberated . . . even if we still live under conditions with little cause for rejoicing." (*Theology and Joy*, p. 50)

56 From "A Mighty Fortress is Our God."

57 This is the joy which Madeleine L'Engle sees captured in the Sanskrit word, *ananda*: "that joy in existence, without which the universe will fall apart and collapse." Madeleine L'Engle, *A Swiftly Tilting Planet* (New York, NY: Dell Publishing, 1979), p. 40. It is the joy that binds Being to being, and all created things to each other. It is the aim of creation and redemption alike.

John Calvin wrote:

> [The] Psalmist calls upon irrational things themselves, the trees, the earth, the seas, and the heavens, to join in the general joy. Nor are we to understand that by the heavens he means the angels, and by the earth men; for he calls even upon the dumb fishes of the deep to shout for joy. . . . As all elements in the creation groan and travail together with us, according to Paul's declaration, (Rom. 8:22) they may reasonably rejoice in the restoration of all things according to their earnest desire.

John Calvin, *Commentary on the Book of Psalms*, trans. Rev. James Anderson (Grand Rapids, MI: Baker BookHouse, reprint, 1979), Vol. IV, p. 58.

58 Quoted in Moltmann, *Theology and Joy*, p. 57.

59 Cornelius Plantinga writes:

> The prophets knew how many ways human life can go wrong because they knew how many ways human life can go right. (You need the concept of a wall on a plumb to tell when one is off.) These prophets kept dreaming of a time when God would put things right again.
>
> They dreamed of a new age in which human crookedness would be straightened out, rough places made plain. The foolish would be made wise and the wise, humble. They dreamed of a time when the deserts would flower, the mountains would run with wine, weeping would cease and people could go to sleep without weapons on their laps. People would work in peace and work to fruitful effect. Lambs could lie down with lions. All nature would be fruitful, benign, and filled with wonder upon wonder; all humans would be knit together in brotherhood and sisterhood; and all nature and all humans would look to God, walk with God, lean toward God and delight in God. Shouts of joy and recognition would well up from valleys and seas, from women in streets and from men on ships.
>
> The webbing together of God, humans, and all creation in justice, fulfillment, and delight is what the Hebrew prophets call *shalom*. We call it peace, but it means far

> more than mere peace of mind or a cease-fire between enemies. In the Bible shalom means *universal flourishing, wholeness, and delight* – a rich state of affairs in which natural needs are satisfied and natural gifts are fruitfully employed, a state of affairs that inspires joyful wonder as its Creator and Savior opens doors and welcomes the creatures in whom he delights. Shalom, in other words, is the way things ought to be.

Cornelius Plantinga, Jr., *Not the Way It's Supposed to Be: A Breviary of Sin*, (Grand Rapids, MI: William B. Eerdmans Publishing Company, 1995), pp. 9-10.

Chapter 5: Joy and the Word of God, Part 1

1 *The Table Talk of Martin Luther*, ed., Thomas S. Kepler (Grand Rapids: Baker Book House, 1952, reprint., 1979), p. 15.

2 See also:

> Blessed is the man
> who walks not in the counsel of the wicked,
> nor stands in the way of sinners,
> nor sits in the seat of scoffers;
> but his delight is in the law of the LORD,
> and on his law he meditates day and night. (Psalm 1:1-2)
> The law of the LORD is perfect,
> reviving the soul;
> the testimony of the LORD is sure,
> making wise the simple;
> the precepts of the LORD are right,
> rejoicing the heart . . .
> More to be desired are they than gold,
> even much fine gold;
> sweeter also than honey
> and drippings of the honeycomb. (Psalm 19:7-10)

3 In my view, it is a mistake to think of distinct faculties as if they were separate from and independent of each other but somehow exist together in the same person. They are woven together in a single fabric. We are intellectual, emotional, volitional beings. Our health and ability to flourish in life are linked to these three dimensions of our inner life working in harmony.

4 William Alston writes:

> Thus we are not afraid of *x* unless we take *x* to be dangerous; we are not angry at *x* unless we take *x* to be acting contrary to something we want; we do not have remorse over having done *x* unless we regard it as unfortunate that we did *x*; we are not grief-stricken over *x* unless we see *x* as the loss of something we wanted very much; we do not have pity for *x* unless we take *x* to be in an undesirable state; and so on.

William P. Alston, "Emotion and Feeling," in *The Encyclopedia of Philosophy*, ed., Paul Edwards (New York: Macmillan Publishing Co., 1967), Vol. II, pp. 479ff.

5 Robert C. Roberts, *Spirituality and Human Emotion*, (Grand Rapids: Williams B. Eerdmans Publishing Co., 1982), p. 26.

6 Louis Pojman has written, "All experiencing takes place within the framework of a world view. . . . What we see depends to some degree on our background beliefs and our expectations. The farmer, the real estate agent, and the artist looking at the "same" field do not see the *same* field." See his article, "A Critique of Gutting's Argument from Religious Experience" in Louis P. Pojman, ed., *Philosophy of Religion: An Anthology* (Belmont, CA: Wadsworth Publishing Co., 1987), pp. 139-140.

7 Roberts contends that emotions "are no less tied to concepts than arguments and beliefs are." *Spirituality*, pp.10, 21. It is also important to affirm the other side of the coin, that emotions are central to worldviews (in the way they actually function in our lives). We are cognitive and affective beings, and the two are woven together. We are more than thinking beings (Descartes); there is no such thing as reason alone (Kant).

8 Roberts also writes that "The Christian emotions . . . (e.g., love, joy, peace) are ways of 'seeing' which are determined by the peculiar Christian concepts and the scheme of beliefs which give rise to those concepts." Ibid., p. 10. And, "They are "concerned ways of viewing things through the 'lenses' of Christian teaching." Ibid., p. 25.

9 Paul L. Holmer, "Blessedness" in *Baker's Dictionary of Christian Ethics*, ed., Carl F.H. Henry (Grand Rapids: Baker Book House Co., 1973), p. 66.

Jonathan Edwards wrote, "Holy affections are not heat without light; but evermore arise from some information of the understanding, some spiritual instruction that the mind receives, some light or actual knowledge." Jonathan Edwards, "On Religious Affections" in *The Works of Jonathan Edwards,* Perry Miller, Gen. ed., (New Haven: Yale University Press, 1959), Vol. 2, p. 281.

10 Roberts writes, "The gospel message provides people with a distinctive way of construing the world; the maker of the universe is your personal loving Father and has redeemed you from sin and death." Roberts, *Spirituality,* p. 16.

11 Josef Pieper, *About Love,* trans., Richard and Clara Winston (Chicago: Franciscan Herald Press, 1974), p. 73. Before him, Aquinas called joy the "delight which follows reason." Thomas Aquinas, *Summa Theologica,* trans. Fathers of the English Dominican Province (London: Burns Oates & Washburn, Ltd., third ed. 1941), I, II, Q. 31, A. 3. I would only add that joy follows reason when reason is illumined by theological insight.

12 This paragraph was written first in Chapter 8 of my *Path of Life: Finding the Joy You've Always Longed For* (Bloomington, IN: WestBow Press, 2015). The fact that joy is perspectival does not make it merely subjective. The fact that we can and do experience joy is evidence that the perspective is true! It fits the world that we live in.

13 This is not to say that we can't learn truth about God-in-his-self-disclosure outside the Scriptures. We can, and it is glorious! Whatever is learned there, however, is learned more fully and clearly in the inspired Word. Many of the truths that frame and fill our joy can only be found here.

14 Romans 15:13

15 God's Word to us includes, but is more than, the Scriptures. The Bible itself tells us that God speaks in many ways, (Hebrews 1:1-2), and records a great variety of ways in which God has spoken over the millennia. In Paul's paradigmatic example of faith in his letter to the Romans (chapter 4), Abraham responds to God's word to him, hundreds of years before sacred scribes began their work. The principle, however, is the same in every age: Faith embraces God's Word – however it comes to us – with an affirming, trusting heart. Therein lies joy.

16 Sometimes, in this fallen world, joy and the discovery of truth have a different relationship. What if the truth you discover is that you have cancer and have one year to live? There is still joy to be found here, but it will lie in discovering the greater truths of what God is seeking to do in and through this crisis, in his presence with you as you walk through the valley of the shadow of death, and in Paul's insight: "For this light momentary affliction is preparing for us an eternal weight of glory beyond all comparison." (2 Corinthians 4:17)

17 Augustine, "The Confessions" in *Basic Writings of Saint Augustine*, ed., Whitney J. Oates (Grand Rapids: Baker Book House, 1980), Vol. I, p. 164. I have changed the King James pronouns and verbal endings to a contemporary form.

18 This is the deeper truth behind Paul's statement that love "rejoices with the truth." (1 Corinthians 13:6)

19 C.S. Lewis, *Letters to Malcolm: Chiefly on Prayer* (New York: Harcourt, Brace & World, Inc.: 1964), pp. 89-90.

20 It was the hubris of the Enlightenment to think that we can reason our way objectively and certainly to truth about the world. It is the hubris of postmodernism to think that truth is entirely the construction of a community, and entirely relative to it.

21 See Arthur F. Holmes, *All Truth is God's Truth* (Grand Rapids: William B. Eerdmans Publishing Co., 1977).

22 Augustine "Teaching Christianity" in *The Works of Saint Augustine: A Translation for the 21st Century*, ed. John E. Rotelle, O.S.A., trans. Edmund Hill, O.P. (New York: New City Press, 1996), I/11, p. 144.

23 John Calvin, *Institutes of the Christian Religion*, trans. Henry Beveridge (Grand Rapids: William B. Eerdmans Publishing Co., eighth print., 1979), Vol. I, pp. 40-41.

24 Ibid., p. 236.

25 John Calvin, *Institutes of the Christian Religion*, ed., John T. McNeill, trans. Ford Lewis Battles (Philadelphia: Westminster, 1960), Vol. 1, p. 82.

26 This is the literal rendering of the Greek word, *theopneustos*, usually translated, "inspired by God" in 2 Timothy 3:16.

27 It was the error of Neo-orthodoxy to limit revelation to the personal disclosure of God. "God in his Word does not speak 'something true,' but himself . . ." And "what God wills to give us cannot really be given in words, but only in manifestation. . . ."Emil Brunner, *Truth As Encounter* (Philadelphia: The Westminster Press, 1964), pp. 132, 131. It is the Fundamentalist error to limit biblical revelation to propositional truth. Both camps are right in what they embrace and wrong in what they exclude.

Revelation is no bare incursion of the Transcendent into the realm of space and time. If it were it would have no meaning for us. It would not be a *personal* encounter, but impersonal. According to Colin Brown:

> It is true that our personalities cannot be compressed into propositions. It is also true that unless we express ourselves in language, our attempts to express ourselves become a dumb charade. To deprive a person of language and the capacity to make himself articulate is to make that person sub-personal. There is no *a priori* reason why the personal God should not be able to express Himself in personal language. And the biblical writers attest this.

Quoted in Ronald H. Nash, *The Word of God and the Word of Man* (Grand Rapids: Zondervan Publishing House, 1982), p. 46.

It is in the propositional dimension of revelation that God sovereignly and graciously supplies us with the meaning of his self-disclosure. It is an equal and opposite error to reduce biblical revelation to bare propositions, however significant they may be. That would indeed be "bibliolatry," as detractors of evangelical Christianity often allege.

28 Acts 7:38

29 1 Peter 1:23

30 Emille Cailliet, *Journey into Light* (Grand Rapids: Zondervan Publishing House, 1968), p. 18.

Ronald Nash gives this very relevant word of caution to evangelical Christians:

> God's revelation is not static or dead; it is a gracious *act* of God. Evangelicals must beware lest their emphasis on revelation inscripturated in human language should degenerate into a de-emphasis of the living and active nature of God's speaking. The God whose voice can raise the dead is not one who can be limited by "dead" words. The activity of the Spirit of God insures the vitality of God's revelation. God speaks and His word is recorded. He continues to speak through that record; and those words live, energized by the Spirit of God.

Ronald Nash, *The Word of God and the Mind of Man*, p. 52.

31 Donald G. Bloesch, *A Theology of Word and Spirit* (Downers Grove, Illinois: InterVarsity Press, 1992), pp. 13-14.

32 J.I. Packer wrote:

> The joy of Bible study is not the fun of collecting esoteric tidbits about Gog and Magog, Tubal-cain and Methuselah, Bible numerics and the beast, and so on. . . . Rather, it is the deep contentment that comes of communing with the living Lord into whose presence the Bible takes us – a joy which only His own true disciples know.

J.I. Packer, *God Has Spoken* (Downers Grove: InterVarsity Press, 1979), p. 10.

33 The spiritual discipline of meditation includes more than a deep reflection on the Scriptures. We can meditate on God himself (Psalm 63:6; 145:5), his works in creation (Psalm 143:5), his deeds in history (including our own lives Psalm 77:12; 119:27; 143:5), as well as on anything that is true, honorable, just, pure, lovely, commendable, excellent, and praiseworthy (Philippians 4:8).

In this chapter my interest is in meditation on the Word of God. Here are a few passages that teach the practice of biblical meditation:

> This Book of the Law shall not depart from your mouth, but you shall meditate on it day and night, so that you may be careful to do according to all that is written in it. For then you will make your way prosperous, and then you will have good success. (Joshua 1:8)
>
> But his delight is in the law of the LORD, and on his law he meditates day and night. (Psalm 1:2)
>
> I will meditate on your precepts and fix my eyes on your ways. (Psalm 119:15)
>
> Even though princes sit plotting against me, your servant will meditate on your statutes. (Psalm 119:23)

34 "Behold, you delight in truth in the inward being,
and you teach me wisdom in the secret heart." (Psalm 51:6)

35 Edwards, "On Religious Affections" in *The Works of Jonathan Edwards*, Vol. 2, p. 272.

36 "And do not be conformed to this world, but be transformed by the renewing of your mind, so that you may prove what the will of God is, that which is good and acceptable and perfect." (Romans 12:2, NASB)

37 See the hymn, "Break Thou the Bread of Life," by Mary A. Lathbury.

38 Walter C. Kaiser, Jr., "What is Biblical Meditation?" in *Renewing Your Mind in a Secular World*, ed., John D. Woodbridge (Chicago: Moody Press, 1985), 50.

CHAPTER 6: JOY AND THE WORD OF GOD, PART 2

1 Most importantly, let me encourage you to develop a consistent practice of reading the Scriptures interactively. Train yourself to ask questions like these as you read:

- Is there worship for me to join?
- Is there a prayer for me to offer?
- Is there a promise for me to embrace?
- Is there a blessing for which I can be thankful?
- Is there a truth for me to affirm?
- Is there wisdom for me to make my own?
- Is there a sin for me to avoid?
- Is there a vice for me to resist?
- Is there a command for me to obey?
- Is there a virtue for me to cultivate?

Lists like this have circulated in various forms for years. This list of questions is one I created for my own ministry of discipleship.

2 "Divine reading" or "Spiritual reading." Although I draw from classic forms of *lectio divina*, this chapter reflects ways in which I have practiced and experienced them in relevant and fruitful ways.

3 Protestant Christians may be surprised to learn that *lectio divina* developed as a tradition in the Roman Catholic Church, inspired by Saint Benedict.

For helpful studies, see the following: David G. Benner, *Opening to God: Lectio Divina and Life as Prayer* (Downers Grove, IL: IVP Books, 2010); Christine Valters Paintner, Lucy Wynkoop, OSB, *Lectio Divina: Contemplative Awakening and Awareness* (New York, Mahwah, NJ: 2008); M. Basil Pennington, *Lectio Divina: Renewing the Ancient Practice of Praying the Scriptures* (New York: Cross Road Publishing, 1998); Raymond Studzinski, *Reading to Live: The Evolving Practice of Lectio Divina*, (Collegeville, MN: Liturgical Press, 2009.

See also: Richard J. Foster, with Kathryn A. Helmers, *Life with God: Reading the Bible for Spiritual Transformation* (New York, NY: HarperCollins, 2008); Evan B. Howard, *Praying the Scriptures: A Field Guide for Your Spiritual Journey* (Downers Grove, IL: InterVarsity Press, 1999); Eugene H. Peterson, *Eat This Book: A Conversation in the Art of Spiritual Reading* (Grand Rapids, MI: Wm. P. Eerdmans Publishing Co., 2006); Peter Toon, *The Art of Meditating on Scripture: Understanding Your Faith, Renewing*

Your Mind, Knowing Your God (Grand Rapids, MI: Zondervan Publishing House, 1993).

4 Because of the time commitment involved in doing a full *lectio divina*, it may be something you do on special occasions to supplement your daily interaction in the Word. However, the more adept you become with this discipline, the more you will be able to practice parts in many different settings, with much time or little.

The spiritual art and discipline of *lectio divina* is framed by an indispensable set of convictions. The first is that the Bible is the Word of God. It belongs to him. It is from him. It serves his purposes for our lives. The second is that the Spirit who inspired the Scriptures in history speaks through them to us today. The third is that God not only speaks to us through his Word, he seeks to commune with us through his Word. The fourth is that God may speak to us through his Word, and manifest his presence through the Word, in any number of ways, none of which we control. The fifth is that God intends to use all of this to make us more like Christ. We can, and should, cultivate these convictions.

There is a matching set of heart-dispositions that must be present for *lectio divina* to be fruitful in our lives. The first is a hunger and thirst to know God, to know his will, and to know his ways. The second is an unreserved yieldedness to the Spirit who inspired the Word and who dwells within us. The third is an eagerness to hear from God, but a willingness to wait in silence for his voice. The fourth is a radical openness to be addressed by God, to meet with God, in whatever way he chooses. The fifth is a resolve to act on whatever God shows us in ways that will make us more like Christ.

5 1 Timothy 4:13. This puts us in a better position to understand Paul's words: "So faith comes from *hearing*, and hearing through the word of Christ." (Romans 10:17)

Reading-as-listening reminds us of the importance of Christian community. While you can and should read and interact with the Scriptures on your own as you cultivate your life with God, it should complement time spent with others in a community of faith. It is good for you to hear others read God's Word, whether it is in the liturgy of a worship service or a group Bible study.

6 Hebrews 1:1, RSV.

7 The Bible itself records many ways and instances in which God communicates with his people apart from the Scriptures. Because of who God is in his absolute truthfulness and unwavering trustworthiness, whatever he communicates apart from his written Word will never contradict or be incompatible with what he has spoken in his written Word. The written Word is the standard against which everything else must be measured. The advantage of listening for the voice of God in *lectio divina* is that it is grounded in and tethered to the written Word.

We should also be very clear that God's communication to us today does not have the status of divine revelation in the Scriptures. The canon is closed. Let none of this, however, deny the reality or diminish the significance of God speaking to his people today. He can and does!

8 Valters Paintner, Wynkoop, *Lectio Divina*, p. 6.

9 Matthew 4:4. We should not miss the fact that Jesus was able to respond to temptation with this Scripture because he likely had meditated on it so often that it came quickly to mind and quickly to his tongue.

10 All Scripture is inspired by God, but not all Scripture has the same purpose. It is a Story, not a collection of timeless axioms. It is the narrative of Redemptive History, which includes many stories of human failure and folly along the way, and much that is background to the Story – the import of which may escape us in our place in history.

To use a metaphor used by Jesus, much of Scripture is like a field in which treasure is buried (Matthew 13:44). Meditation honors the earth that holds the treasure, but seeks the gems that enrich our lives. I don't know, for instance, that the genealogies in the Bible will be fruitful for meditation, but they point to a greater truth that is worthy of our meditation: "When the fullness of time had come, God sent forth his Son, born of woman, born under the law, to redeem those who were under the law." (Galatians 4:3-5)

We have exactly what God wanted us to have in the Bible. We should approach every page with a reverent and thankful heart. In all our reading we should seek the face of God and listen for the voice of God. It is not at all irreverent, however, or errant theology, to recognize that not all Scripture speaks in the same way.

Jesus said that the Scriptures testify to him (John 5:39), and find their fulfillment in him (Luke 24:24-32). If we seek Christ in our meditation, and prayerfully read everything through the lens of the Gospel, the Spirit of God will speak to us through the Word of God.

11 In Latin, *oratio* is a speech. In your *oratio*, you are speaking to God.

12 In Luke 22:42 Jesus prayed, "Father, if you are willing, take this cup from me; yet not my will, but yours be done."

13 1 Samuel 3:9, NIV.

14 "Let my prayer be counted as incense before you, and the lifting up of my hands as the evening sacrifice." (Psalm141:2)

15 "In the same way, the Spirit helps us in our weakness. We do not know what we ought to pray for, but the Spirit himself intercedes for us through wordless groans. And he who searches our hearts knows the mind of the Spirit, because the Spirit intercedes for God's people in accordance with the will of God." (Romans 8:26-27)

16 *Contemplatio* signifies looking at, gazing at, surveying. This is so, even if it involves ideas and our "mind's eye." According to The Oxford Latin Dictionary, *contemplatio* refers first to "The action of looking at, regarding, view." Its cognate, *contemplo* means "To look at hard, examine visually, gaze at." The *Oxford Latin Dictionary*, ed., P.G.W. Glare (Oxford: Clarendon Press, reprint 1983), pp. 426-27.

17 See, for example:

> My eyes are ever toward the LORD, for he will pluck my feet out of the net. (Psalm 25:15)
>
> But my eyes are toward you, O God, my Lord; in you I seek refuge; leave me not defenseless! (Psalm 141:8)
>
> For this reason, because I have heard of your faith in the Lord Jesus and your love toward all the saints, I do not cease to give thanks for you, remembering you in my prayers, that the God of our Lord Jesus Christ, the Father of glory, may give you the Spirit of wisdom and of revelation in the knowledge of him, having the eyes of your hearts enlightened. . . (Ephesians 1:15-18)

18 Calvin said that in the Scriptures God "lisps with us as nurses are wont to do with little children." John Calvin, *Institutes of the Christian Religion*, trans. Henry Beveridge (Grand Rapids, MI: William B. Eerdmans Publishing Co., eighth printing, 1979), 1.13.1.

19 2 Corinthians 5:13-15

20 2 Corinthians 5:16-17

Made in the USA
Columbia, SC
16 February 2018